SEE & EXPLORE
LIBRARY

MACHINES

·AND·HOW·THEY·

·WORK·

Written by
David Burnie

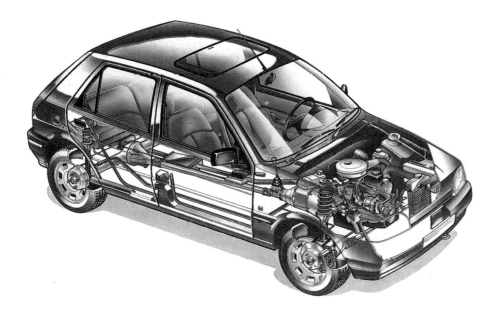

DORLING KINDERSLEY

NEW YORK

A Dorling Kindersley Book

Editor Miranda Smith
Art editor Chris Scollen

Managing art editor Roger Priddy

Series editor Angela Wilkes
Editorial director Sue Unstead
Production controller Louise Barratt

Contributing illustrators
Aziz Khan and Simon Roulstone,
Jason Lewis, Robert Walster and Sean Wilkinson
Gerald Wood, Mick Gillah, Hussein Hussein

First American Edition, 1991

10 9 8 7 6 5 4 3 2

Dorling Kindersley Inc., 232 Madison
Avenue, New York, New York 10016

Copyright © 1991 Dorling Kindersley
Limited, London

ISBN 1-879431-15-7
ISBN 1-879431-30-0 (lib.bdg.)

Library of Congress Catalog Card Number 91-060147

Phototypeset by SX Composing, Essex
Colour Separations by DOT Gradations Limited
Printed in Spain by Artes Graficas, Toledo S.A.
D.L.TO:2141-1991

CONTENTS

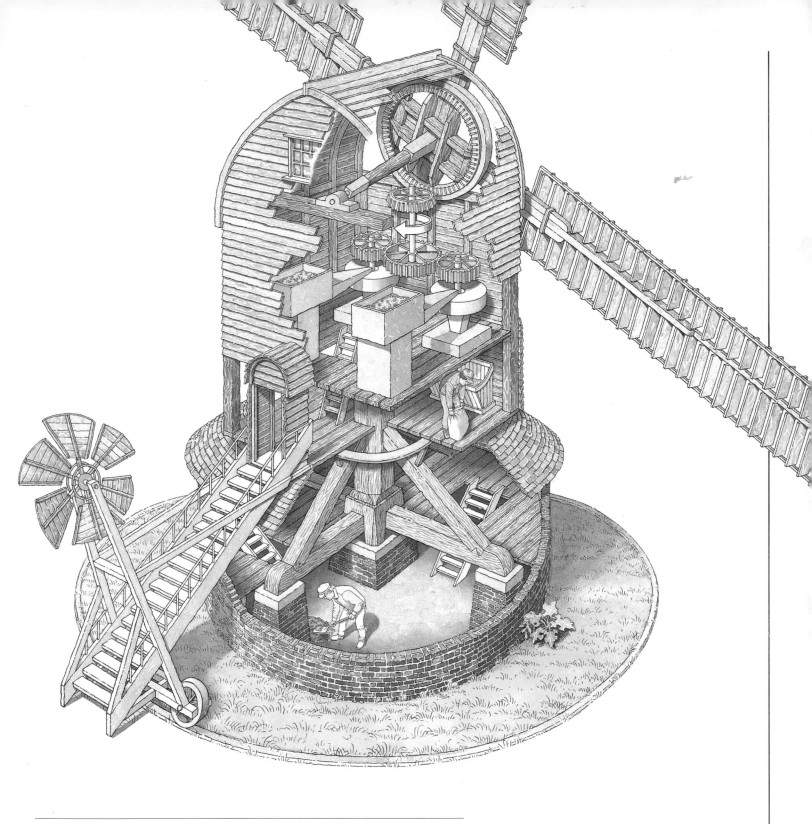

WHAT IS A MACHINE?

A machine is a device that has been built to do a job. Machines have a number of different parts, and these are arranged to work together to do something useful. The earliest machines had only a few parts (pages 8–9). Many of today's machines are much more complicated.

This book is mainly about mechanical machines – ones that convert one sort of movement into another. When you ride a bicycle, for example, your feet go round and round but the bicycle moves forward in a straight line. A windmill works the other way around. It converts the movement of the wind – in a straight line – into the movement of grindstones, which turn round and round. Simple machines, like the bicycle, are powered by muscles. Many of the machines in this book are powered not by muscles but by fuel. Fuels such as coal, oil and gasoline contain energy that is locked up. Energy is released when the fuels are burned. It produces more power for movement, making it possible to perform certain tasks faster.

An age of machines

In a day, you might use dozens of different machines, for cooking food, telling the time, entertaining yourself, or for getting about. Many specialized machines are also used in factories, in the air, or in the sea. Some produce things we need, and some make other machines. Without machines, our lives would be unimaginably different!

Trains

These were the first machines to make fast, long-distance travel possible. Today, they reach speeds of up to 236mph (380km/h). More about trains on pages 20–23.

Bicycles

Like trains and cars, bicycles use wheels and bearings to reduce friction. Together, these help to make sure that as much energy as possible is turned into forward movement. More about bicycles on pages 18–19.

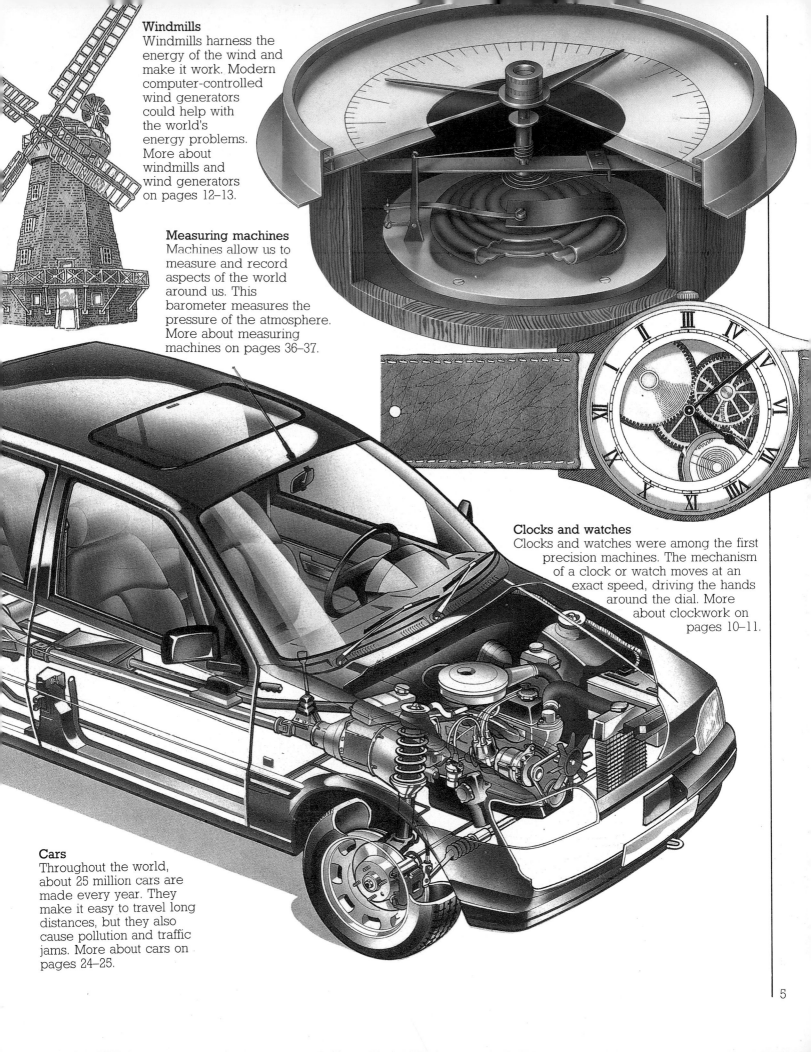

Windmills
Windmills harness the energy of the wind and make it work. Modern computer-controlled wind generators could help with the world's energy problems. More about windmills and wind generators on pages 12–13.

Measuring machines
Machines allow us to measure and record aspects of the world around us. This barometer measures the pressure of the atmosphere. More about measuring machines on pages 36–37.

Clocks and watches
Clocks and watches were among the first precision machines. The mechanism of a clock or watch moves at an exact speed, driving the hands around the dial. More about clockwork on pages 10–11.

Cars
Throughout the world, about 25 million cars are made every year. They make it easy to travel long distances, but they also cause pollution and traffic jams. More about cars on pages 24–25.

MUSCLE POWER

We know exactly who invented modern machines such as the car, the vacuum cleaner, and the telephone. But we will never know who invented the first machines. These people lived thousands of years ago, long before writing was known about, and their names have long since been forgotten.

However, we do know for certain that in order to make the very first machines people needed tools. These tools were very simple. They included sharp stones, which were used for cutting, and long branches, for moving heavy rocks. It was only when tools like these had been in use for a very long time that the first machines appeared.

The machines and devices used by our distant ancestors all relied on muscle power. To begin with, many people had to work together to move heavy objects. But when animals such as oxen were domesticated, their muscles could be used too. This was a great step forward, because it meant that machines could be made much bigger.

Relying on Nature
The first machines were made out of whatever natural materials people could find, such as stones, logs, branches, and plant fibers. Many years were to pass before the discovery of metals brought about their use in machines.

The roller
The log roller was one of the earliest mechanical devices. It worked by reducing friction. Long ago, people found that while it was very difficult to move a heavy object that was sitting on the ground, it would move quite easily if rollers were placed underneath. Log rollers enabled the ancient Egyptians to move the heavy blocks of stone that they used in building the pyramids.

The fiddle borer

The fiddle borer was used by our ancestors to light fires. The "fiddle" was a thin piece of skin stretched between the ends of a flexible stick. The skin was looped around another stick, which was held upright in a pile of dry leaves. When the fiddle was pulled backward and forward, the upright stick turned very quickly. Friction made the end of the stick get hot enough to set fire to the leaves.

The shaduf
The shaduf is a kind of crane used for lifting water. It consists of a strong wooden pole strapped to wooden legs. At one end of the pole is a bucket, and at the other end is a pile of stones held together by rope. The bucket is pulled down and dipped into the water. When it is full, the farmer lets go and the bag rises, lifted by the weight of the stones. The bag is then emptied into a trough.

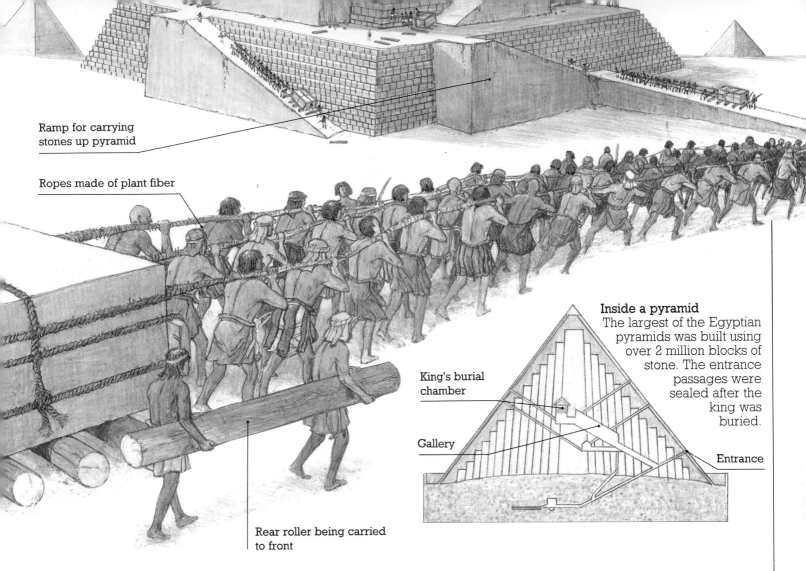

Ramp for carrying
stones up pyramid

Ropes made of plant fiber

Rear roller being carried
to front

Inside a pyramid
The largest of the Egyptian
pyramids was built using
over 2 million blocks of
stone. The entrance
passages were
sealed after the
king was
buried.

King's burial
chamber

Gallery

Entrance

The plow

The wheel

Plows have been used for at least 5,000 years. They break up ground and turn it over so that crops can be grown. The first plows were little more than sticks. Early farmers pushed or dragged them through the ground using their own muscle power. When oxen started to be used in farming, plows became bigger and heavier. This meant that they could dig deeper into the ground.

The wheel was invented sometime before 3000 BC. The first wheels were solid and made of a number of planks of wood arranged side by side and shaped into a circle. Wheels like this are strong but heavy. The invention of spokes made wheels lighter without any loss of strength. The wheel is one of the most important inventions. Strangely, it was unknown in the New World until the arrival of Europeans.

EARLY INVENTIONS

With the right materials and enough time, you could probably build any of the machines on the previous two pages yourself. But as technology advanced, machines grew more complicated, and making them became a job that was carried out by craftsmen who made machines like the ones shown here. These were all used or designed in the more recent past, between about 2,000 and 500 years ago. You would have difficulty in making any of these machines yourself, because their parts have to fit together exactly if the machine is to work. You would need special tools, and

experience in shaping wood and metal.

The machines shown here have features that are still of great importance in the machines we use today. The screw, which is used in the Archimedean screw and the printing press, allows a lot of force to be applied when it is turned. Gears, which are used in the south-pointing carriage, allow movement to be sped up or slowed down and carried between different points in the machine. Bearings, which are used by all these machines, allow them to run smoothly without losing too much energy.

Making things move

With one exception, the machines shown here all rely on muscle power to make them work. The one that does not is Hero's aeolipile. It turns chemical energy into movement by burning a fuel. This makes it a forerunner of all the powered machines we use today.

The Archimedean screw

The Archimedean screw is an ingenious wooden pump invented over 2,000 years ago. When the handle is turned, water is lifted up inside the cylindrical case by the screw. When the water

reaches the top, it pours out of an opening and flows away. This kind of pump is named after the Greek scientist Archimedes, who lived between 287 and 212 BC. No one is really sure if he actually invented it.

Handle

Water flows out here

Wooden case

Screw

Water flows in here

8

The first steam engine

Nozzle

Spinning sphere

Water tank

The first steam-powered machine was invented in the first century AD by the Greek mathematician, Hero of Alexandria. Hero's "aeolipile," as it was called, consisted of a metal tank of water connected to a metal sphere by two pipes. The water in the tank was heated until it boiled, and steam flowed into the sphere. The steam escaped through two nozzles, making the sphere spin around.

The south-pointing carriage

Statue

Gears inside carriage

This strange machine was invented in China in the third century AD. It consisted of a carriage with a pointing statue on top of it. If the statue was set so that it pointed south, it stayed pointing south no matter which way the carriage was turned. The secret behind the curious statue was a set of gears hidden inside the carriage. They worked much like the gears in a car's differential (pages 24–25).

The printing press

Screw

Printing block

Printing presses were first used by Johannes Gutenberg, who lived between 1400 and 1468. To work the press, a lever was pulled that turned a heavy screw. This forced the printing block down against the paper. Although Gutenberg invented printing, he did not invent the press. Farmers had been using similar machines for hundreds of years to press olives to make olive oil.

Into the future

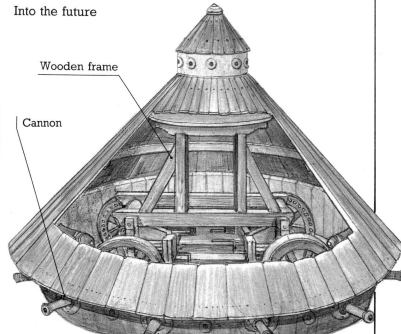

Wooden frame

Cannon

The Italian painter, sculptor, and engineer Leonardo da Vinci designed many machines that were centuries ahead of their time. They included parachutes, helicopters, and this wooden tank. The tank is equipped with cannons and was meant to be pushed along by people inside. Leonardo lived from 1452 to 1519 and sketched his designs in notebooks.

TIME AND MOTION

Mechanical clocks and watches may be different in size, but they work in a very similar way. At the heart of both is a mechanism that moves at an exact speed. In a grandfather clock, this is a pendulum, while in a watch, it is a hairspring.

The principle of the pendulum was discovered hundreds of years ago by the scientist Galileo Galilei. He realized that, as he watched a chandelier swinging from a ceiling, no matter how far it swung, each swing took exactly the same time. Also, the time each swing took depended on the length of the rope.

In a grandfather clock, the pendulum swings backward and forward. Just like Galileo's chandelier, it takes a precise amount of time to complete each swing. The pendulum swings a device called an anchor. The anchor ensures that the cogwheels in the clock move at the right speed, and so the hands tell the time correctly. In a wind-up watch, the hairspring does the same job as the pendulum.

Grandfather clock
A grandfather clock is very tall because it has a long pendulum. This makes it more accurate. The clock is powered by a heavy lead or stone weight that hangs from a rope.

Cogwheels
The clock contains many different cogwheels. They are needed to drive the two hands at different speeds. Each one has a different number of teeth. The complicated combination of cogwheels ensures that the minute hand moves exactly 12 times faster than the hour hand.

Pendulum
The pendulum regulates the speed of the clock by swinging from side to side at a fixed rate. The weight turns the cogwheels, and the movement of the escape wheel and anchor keeps the pendulum swinging.

Keeping time
In some ways, a pendulum clock is like a swing. If you sit on a swing, it always takes you the same time to travel backward and forward, no matter how high you go. The same is true when a pendulum swings. Also, just as a friend can provide you with the force to keep swinging, in a clock, the weight provides the force to keep the pendulum swinging.

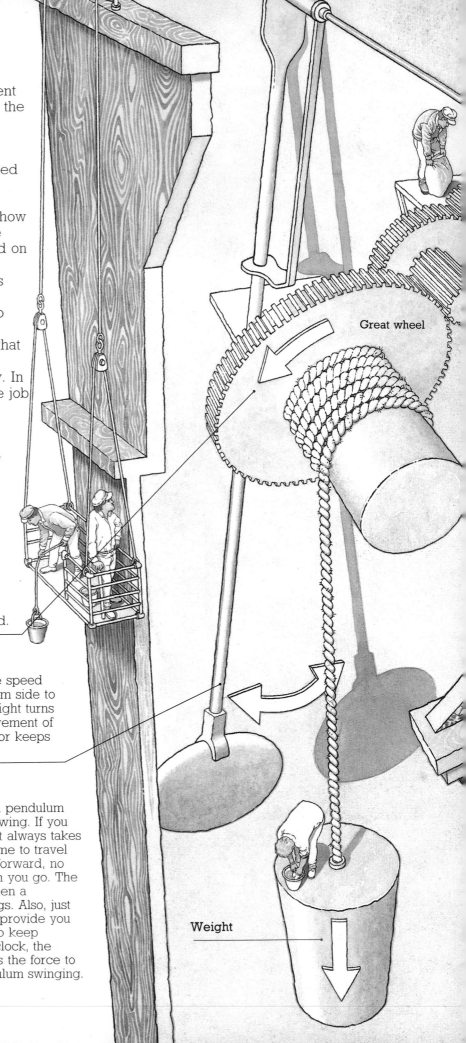

Great wheel

Weight

Anchor

As the anchor swings, its two pallets catch and release the teeth on the escape wheel. This makes the escape wheel turn in time with the pendulum's movement.

Anchor

Pallet

Escape wheel

Hands

Early clocks

The first clocks did not have cogwheels or hands. Instead, they used water, sand, or the movement of the sun to tell the time.

Water clock

This Chinese water clock consists of a container of water with a small hole in it. The water slowly trickles out of the container. The time is told by comparing the water level with marks on the side of the container.

Sundial

The sundial is probably the oldest kind of clock. As the sun moves across the sky, a shadow of the pointer is cast onto a dial. The time can then be seen by looking at the dial. One disadvantage of the sundial is that it does not work on cloudy days.

Hourglass

An hourglass consists of two glass containers joined by a narrow tube. Inside the containers is a precise amount of very fine sand. The sand flows through the tube from the top container to the bottom one. It takes exactly one hour for all the sand to flow through.

Wristwatch

The parts that make up a mechanical wristwatch have to be much smaller than those of a clock. A watch does not have a pendulum. Instead, it is regulated by a device called a hairspring. The hairspring is always winding and unwinding. It does this at a precise rate and is used to regulate the movement of the cogwheels. The watch is powered by a larger spring called the mainspring. This has to be wound up every few days.

Winder

Hands

Face

Mainspring

SAIL POWER

Windmills use the power of the wind to grind grain into flour or to pump water out of fields. At one time, these huge and graceful machines were a common sight in many countries. Today, they have been replaced by gasoline-powered machines and have almost disappeared.

Although wind power is free, it is not very reliable. The wind rarely blows at the same speed for long, and it often changes direction. In early windmills, not much could be done about this. Later on, windmills were improved so they could make the most of the wind. Instead of being fixed in one direction, they were made so that they could be turned to face the wind. In some windmills, the miller would have to turn the mill by hand, but later a device called a fantail was invented, which turned the mill automatically.

Post mill

The windmill shown here is designed for grinding grain. It is a "post" mill, meaning that it is mounted on a central post. It rotates around the post to face into the wind.

Fantail

The fantail makes sure that the main sails always face the right way. When the mill is facing into the wind, the fantail does not turn. But if the wind changes direction, the fantail's blades begin to move. This powers a winding gear that moves the truck wheels. The mill keeps turning until it faces the wind once more, then the fantail stops.

Post

The post is the biggest piece of timber in the whole mill. It needs to be strong to bear the strain when the mill is working in a high wind. The post is supported by a framework of beams. In this mill, the base of the post is enclosed by a circular wall and roof, making a storage area.

Windshaft

The windshaft is a giant wooden axle that supports the sails and the brake wheel. The brake wheel turns the wallower and great spur wheel, which powers the grindstones.

Sail stock

Brake wheel

Spur wheel

Wallower

Grain hopper

Fantail

Truck wheels

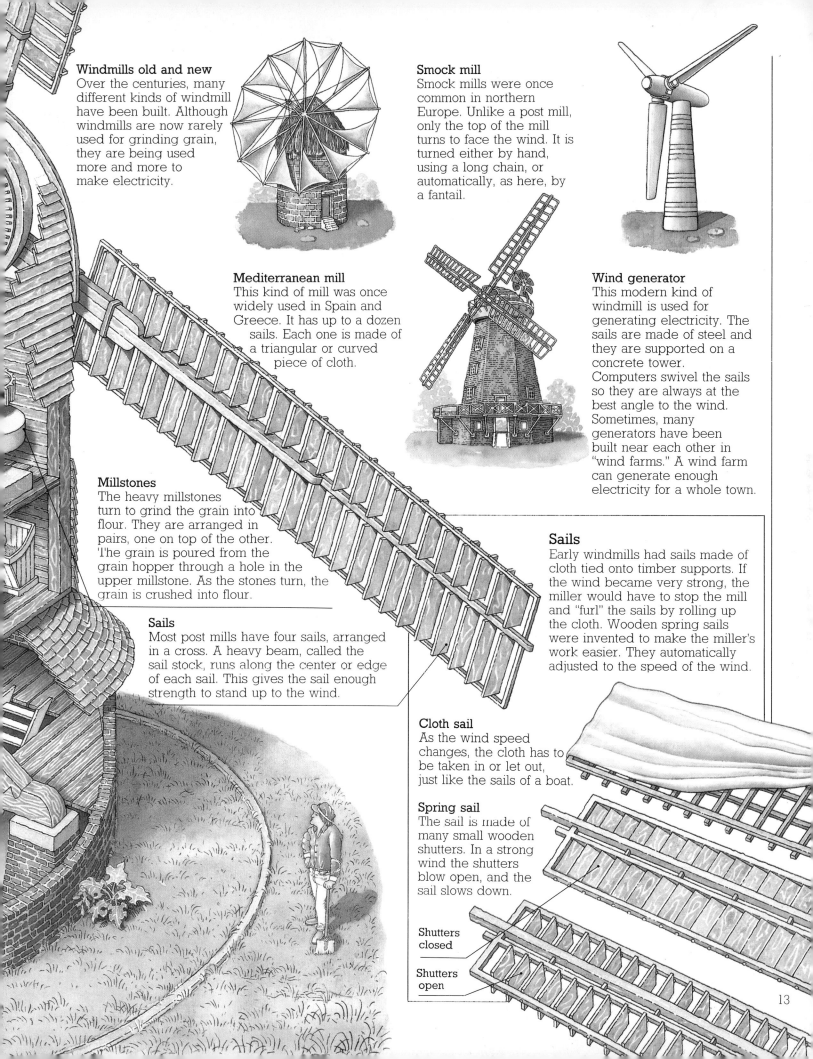

Windmills old and new

Over the centuries, many different kinds of windmill have been built. Although windmills are now rarely used for grinding grain, they are being used more and more to make electricity.

Mediterranean mill

This kind of mill was once widely used in Spain and Greece. It has up to a dozen sails. Each one is made of a triangular or curved piece of cloth.

Smock mill

Smock mills were once common in northern Europe. Unlike a post mill, only the top of the mill turns to face the wind. It is turned either by hand, using a long chain, or automatically, as here, by a fantail.

Wind generator

This modern kind of windmill is used for generating electricity. The sails are made of steel and they are supported on a concrete tower. Computers swivel the sails so they are always at the best angle to the wind. Sometimes, many generators have been built near each other in "wind farms." A wind farm can generate enough electricity for a whole town.

Millstones

The heavy millstones turn to grind the grain into flour. They are arranged in pairs, one on top of the other. The grain is poured from the grain hopper through a hole in the upper millstone. As the stones turn, the grain is crushed into flour.

Sails

Most post mills have four sails, arranged in a cross. A heavy beam, called the sail stock, runs along the center or edge of each sail. This gives the sail enough strength to stand up to the wind.

Sails

Early windmills had sails made of cloth tied onto timber supports. If the wind became very strong, the miller would have to stop the mill and "furl" the sails by rolling up the cloth. Wooden spring sails were invented to make the miller's work easier. They automatically adjusted to the speed of the wind.

Cloth sail

As the wind speed changes, the cloth has to be taken in or let out, just like the sails of a boat.

Spring sail

The sail is made of many small wooden shutters. In a strong wind the shutters blow open, and the sail slows down.

Shutters closed

Shutters open

13

POWER FROM WATER

No one knows exactly when people first had the idea of using the force of flowing water. The Romans had waterwheels for grinding grain, so machines powered by water are at least 2,000 years old. Waterwheels have been used to power many different types of machines and devices. These have included heavy hammers for beating metal and looms for weaving cloth.

Unlike wind power, water power is reliable and fairly easy to harness. It is still used on a large scale throughout the world to generate electricity. The giant water turbines in a hydroelectric power station are the modern equivalent of waterwheels. Their special shape ensures that the water's energy is collected and passed on to the generators. The water needed to turn the turbines is held in dams that are often many hundreds of feet high. At the press of a switch, the sluice gates at the base of a dam can be raised. Water pours into the turbines, and the generators surge to life.

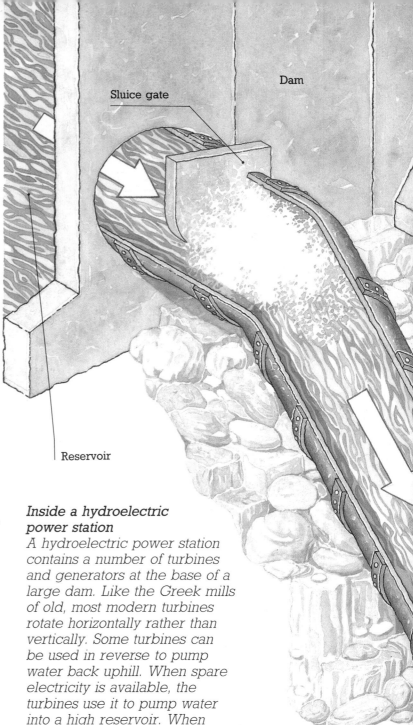

Sluice gate
Dam
Reservoir

Greek mill
The Greek mill is one of the earliest types of waterwheel. Unlike most later waterwheels, it turns horizontally. Water pours out of a wooden chute to strike the wheel's paddles.

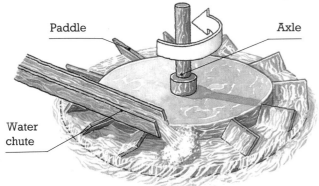

Paddle
Axle
Water chute

Overshot mill
There are two main kinds of waterwheel. In an "overshot" waterwheel, shown here, the water flows over the top of the wheel. The wheel is turned by the weight of the falling water. In an "undershot" waterwheel, the water flows underneath the wheel and pushes its paddles.

Inside a hydroelectric power station
A hydroelectric power station contains a number of turbines and generators at the base of a large dam. Like the Greek mills of old, most modern turbines rotate horizontally rather than vertically. Some turbines can be used in reverse to pump water back uphill. When spare electricity is available, the turbines use it to pump water into a high reservoir. When electricity is needed, the water is allowed to flow back through the turbines, and electricity is produced.

Bucket-like paddles
Stream

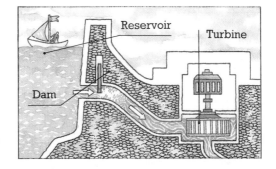

Reservoir
Turbine
Dam

14

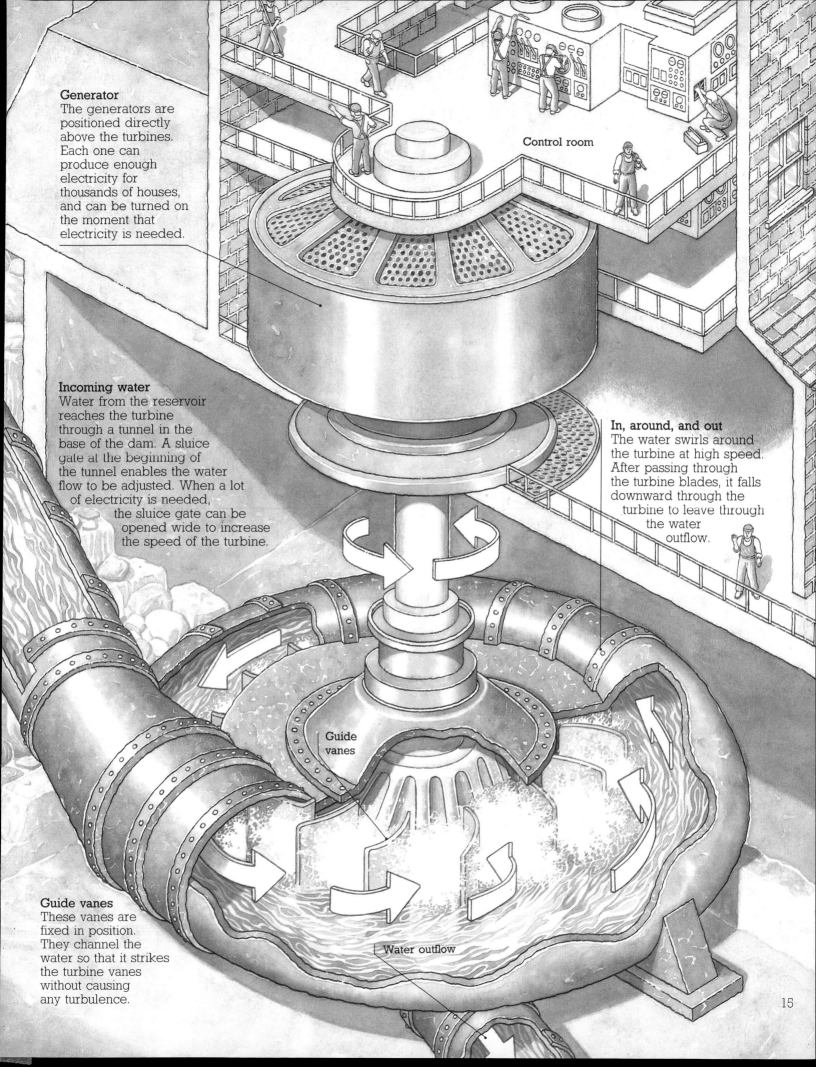

Generator
The generators are positioned directly above the turbines. Each one can produce enough electricity for thousands of houses, and can be turned on the moment that electricity is needed.

Control room

Incoming water
Water from the reservoir reaches the turbine through a tunnel in the base of the dam. A sluice gate at the beginning of the tunnel enables the water flow to be adjusted. When a lot of electricity is needed, the sluice gate can be opened wide to increase the speed of the turbine.

In, around, and out
The water swirls around the turbine at high speed. After passing through the turbine blades, it falls downward through the turbine to leave through the water outflow.

Guide vanes

Guide vanes
These vanes are fixed in position. They channel the water so that it strikes the turbine vanes without causing any turbulence.

Water outflow

15

ALL SEWN UP

If you have ever tried sewing by hand, you will know that it is a slow job that needs a lot of patience. Over the years, machine designers have looked for ways to make sewing faster. The first sewing machines appeared as long ago as the late 1700s, and within a century, they were being made in the millions. When you sew by hand, you use just a single thread, and you work from both sides of the fabric. Each time you make a stitch, you push the needle right through the fabric and out the other side. A sewing machine does not work like this. It has two separate threads. One passes through the eye of the needle, while the other lies under the fabric in a spool or bobbin.

To make a stitch, the machine pushes the needle and its thread through the fabric until a small loop appears on the other side. A hook then catches this loop, and pulls it around the bobbin. The loop then slips off the hook, and is pulled tight. The needle thread pulls the bobbin thread with it, and the result – in a fraction of a second – is a stitch.

Electric sewing machine
Most modern sewing machines are powered by electricity. The electric motor drives the top shaft, and this movement raises and lowers the needle, moves the fabric, and turns the bobbin hook.

Feed-dog
The feed-dog is a device that moves the fabric forward after the machine finishes a stitch. It has two sets of teeth. These grip the fabric when the feed-dog lifts up and forward. After the fabric has been moved, the feed-dog moves down and then back. The length of each stitch depends on how far forward the feed-dog moves.

Driving the needle
A sewing machine's needle does not simply move up and down. It has to pause for a fraction of a second each time it pierces the fabric. It then moves down slightly to make a loop of thread. The different parts of the needle drive mechanism produce this complicated movement.

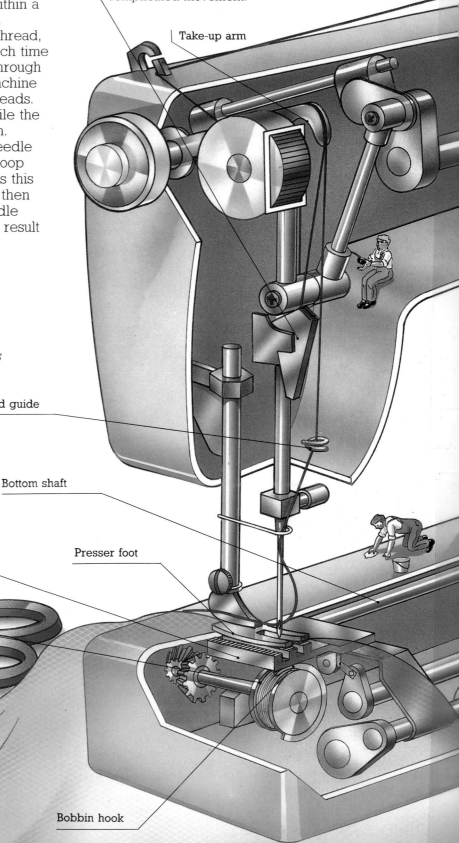

Take-up arm

Thread guide

Bottom shaft

Presser foot

Bobbin

Bobbin hook

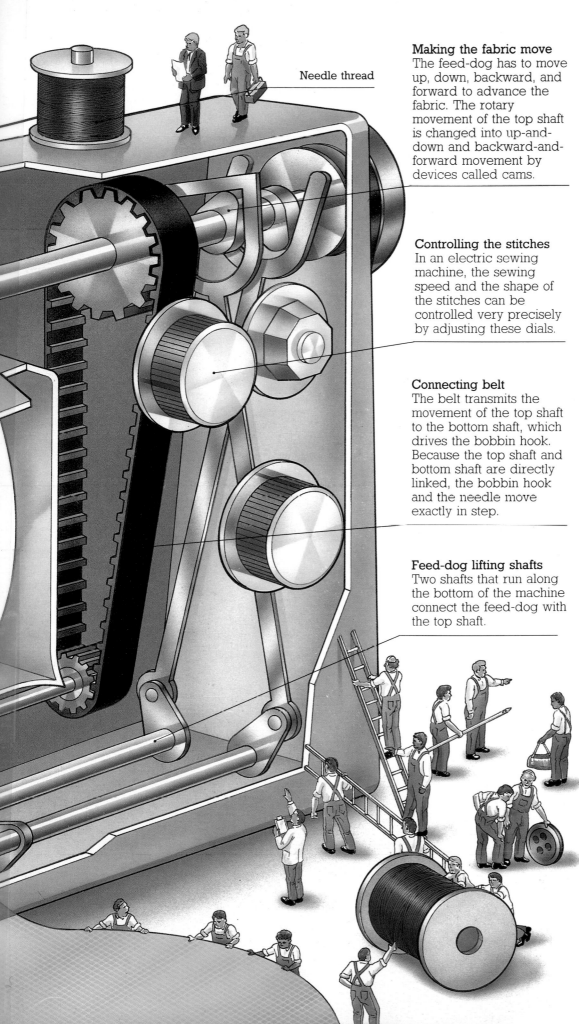

Needle thread

Making the fabric move
The feed-dog has to move up, down, backward, and forward to advance the fabric. The rotary movement of the top shaft is changed into up-and-down and backward-and-forward movement by devices called cams.

Controlling the stitches
In an electric sewing machine, the sewing speed and the shape of the stitches can be controlled very precisely by adjusting these dials.

Connecting belt
The belt transmits the movement of the top shaft to the bottom shaft, which drives the bobbin hook. Because the top shaft and bottom shaft are directly linked, the bobbin hook and the needle move exactly in step.

Feed-dog lifting shafts
Two shafts that run along the bottom of the machine connect the feed-dog with the top shaft.

Making the stitch
To make a stitch, the needle and bobbin hook have to work exactly in time. The needle pushes down through the fabric, and the bobbin hook loops the needle thread around the bobbin.

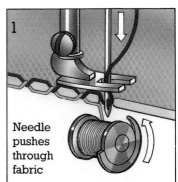

1 Needle pushes through fabric

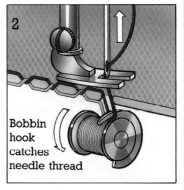

2 Bobbin hook catches needle thread

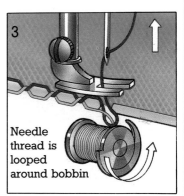

3 Needle thread is looped around bobbin

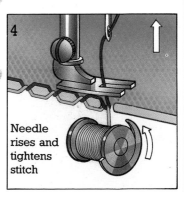

4 Needle rises and tightens stitch

TWO-WHEELED TRAVEL

The bicycle is one of the most successful of all muscle-powered machines. Getting around by bike is easy because you waste little energy battling against friction. A bike's pedals and wheels are mounted on bearings, which means that they turn very easily. When you are traveling downhill, you do not have to pedal at all. You can "freewheel" and let gravity do all the work for you.

The first bicycles were made of wood or iron, and were very heavy. They had solid tires of metal or rubber. Riding them must have been uncomfortable because roads then had very bumpy surfaces. Modern bicycles are much lighter. Air-filled tires give a smooth ride, and gears make light work of hills. In some parts of the world, bicycles are the main form of transport. Unlike cars, they do not need any fuel, and they do not cause pollution.

All-terrain bike

An all-terrain bike, or mountain bike, is specially designed for off-road riding. It is light but strong, and can travel over rough ground that would damage an ordinary bike.

Getting in gear

Most all-terrain bikes have five gear sprockets on the rear wheel and three front chain wheels. Together, they give a total of 15 different gears to choose from.

The bicycle grows up

Over the last 200 years, cycles have become lighter, faster, and much more comfortable.

Saddle

Brakes
Long levers on the handlebars allow the brake cables to be pulled with a lot of force. The brake blocks then press tightly against the wheel rims, which slow the bike down.

Seat tube

Crossbar

Front gear changer

Chain

Chain wheels

Rear gear changer

Hobbyhorse
The hobbyhorse, which was invented in about 1800, had no pedals. To ride it, you sat astride the saddle and pushed with your feet.

Velocipede
One of the earliest pedal cycles, the velocipede, was invented in about 1850. It was also known as the "boneshaker."

Penny farthing
The enormous front wheel of a penny farthing, or "ordinary" bicycle, could be as much as 5 feet (1.5m) in diameter.

Safety cycle, 1885
Made from the mid-1880s, safety cycles had important new features – a chain and air-filled tires for a more comfortable ride.

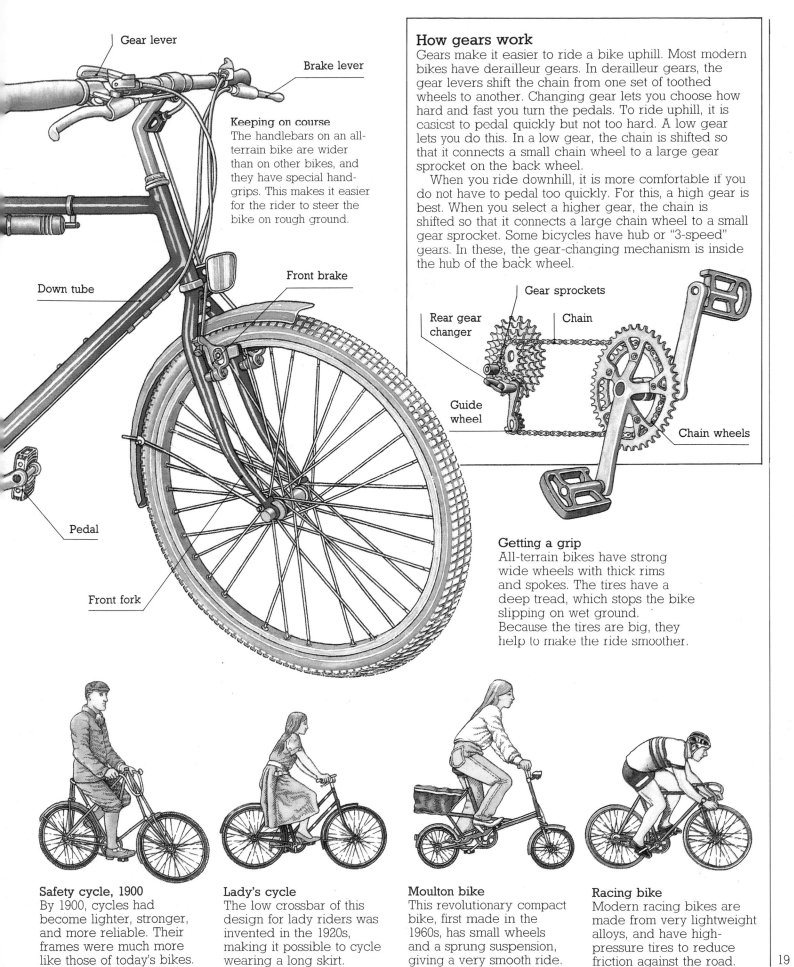

Gear lever

Brake lever

Keeping on course
The handlebars on an all-terrain bike are wider than on other bikes, and they have special hand-grips. This makes it easier for the rider to steer the bike on rough ground.

Down tube

Front brake

Pedal

Front fork

How gears work
Gears make it easier to ride a bike uphill. Most modern bikes have derailleur gears. In derailleur gears, the gear levers shift the chain from one set of toothed wheels to another. Changing gear lets you choose how hard and fast you turn the pedals. To ride uphill, it is easiest to pedal quickly but not too hard. A low gear lets you do this. In a low gear, the chain is shifted so that it connects a small chain wheel to a large gear sprocket on the back wheel.

When you ride downhill, it is more comfortable if you do not have to pedal too quickly. For this, a high gear is best. When you select a higher gear, the chain is shifted so that it connects a large chain wheel to a small gear sprocket. Some bicycles have hub or "3-speed" gears. In these, the gear-changing mechanism is inside the hub of the back wheel.

Gear sprockets

Rear gear changer

Chain

Guide wheel

Chain wheels

Getting a grip
All-terrain bikes have strong wide wheels with thick rims and spokes. The tires have a deep tread, which stops the bike slipping on wet ground. Because the tires are big, they help to make the ride smoother.

Safety cycle, 1900
By 1900, cycles had become lighter, stronger, and more reliable. Their frames were much more like those of today's bikes.

Lady's cycle
The low crossbar of this design for lady riders was invented in the 1920s, making it possible to cycle wearing a long skirt.

Moulton bike
This revolutionary compact bike, first made in the 1960s, has small wheels and a sprung suspension, giving a very smooth ride.

Racing bike
Modern racing bikes are made from very lightweight alloys, and have high-pressure tires to reduce friction against the road.

RUNNING ON RAILS

The first railways were built over 400 years ago. They had wooden rails and wagons, and they were used for hauling coal out of mines. There were no locomotives in those days, so the wagons had to be pushed by hand. The modern railway age was born with the invention of the steam engine. The power of steam had been discovered in the first century AD (*page 9*), but practical steam engines were not invented until 1,700 years later. At first, they were fixed in place and powered pumps to drain water from mines. Later, they were put on wheels and pulled carriages on metal rails.

In their heyday, steam locomotives were the largest and most powerful land vehicles ever made. Railways were built across countries and continents. They helped to open up the Wild West, and they made fast long-distance travel possible for the first time. The world speed record for a steam locomotive was set in 1938 between Grantham and Peterborough in England. With the coal in its firebox burning white-hot, the locomotive *Mallard*, pulling a full train of carriages, reached a speed of 126mph (203km/h).

American locomotives

The locomotives that helped to open up the American West were specially designed for traveling across open country. Wood was plentiful, and the trainmen used this as fuel. The burning wood produced sparks. The spark guard on the chimney trapped the sparks and stopped them from setting fire to the forest alongside the track. The cowcatcher at the front of the locomotive pushed aside wild animals and cattle that strayed onto the track.

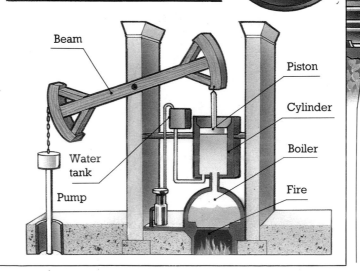

Spark guard

Blast pipe

Leading wheel

Cowcatcher

Newcomen's steam engine

One of the first steam engines was built in England by Thomas Newcomen in 1712. It was used for pumping water out of mines. It had a large wooden beam that swung up and down like a see-saw. The beam was pushed and pulled by a piston inside a cylinder. When steam was let into the cylinder, the piston was pushed upward. Cold water was then sprayed into the cylinder. This turned the steam into water, sucking the piston back down.

Beam

Water tank

Pump

Piston

Cylinder

Boiler

Fire

Cylinder and piston

Steam from the dome is piped to the two cylinders. A sliding valve lets the steam into the cylinder, making it enter the cylinder alternately from the front and the back. The steam pushes the piston backward and forward. Rods connected to the piston drive the wheels.

The *Rocket*

This early steam locomotive was designed by the Englishman George Stephenson. Each of its front wheels was driven by a piston, and it pulled a tender containing coal and water. Running without a train, the *Rocket* could reach a speed of nearly 30mph (48km/h). This made it the first powered machine capable of moving faster than a man on horseback. It pulled some of the world's earliest passenger trains and was famous for winning the world's first steam locomotive race, in 1829.

Safety valve

Steam pipe

Driving wheel

Boiler tubes

The boiler is a large tank filled with water. The hot air and smoke from the firebox are sucked through the boiler in a series of tubes. The tubes get very hot and the water starts to boil, creating the steam. Water has to be added from time to time to keep the boiler topped up.

Dome

Steam from the boiler collects inside the dome. As more and more steam arrives, the pressure inside the dome builds up. When it is high enough, the driver turns a valve that lets the steam flow to the pistons. When this is done, the wheels begin to turn.

Firebox

Unlike an electric or diesel locomotive, a steam locomotive takes quite a bit of time to get going. To raise enough steam, the fireman must shovel coal or wood into the firebox. As the fire heats up, hot air and smoke from the firebox are then sucked forward into the boiler tubes.

Tender

Fuel for the fire is carried in the tender. In Europe there were many mines, so steam locomotives usually burned coal. In America, they burned wood. Wood does not produce as much heat energy as coal. A large tender was needed so a lot of wood could be carried.

21

Picking up speed

The earliest steam locomotives were so slow that a person running could have overtaken them. But since passenger trains first entered service over 150 years ago they have become faster and faster. At first, all locomotives were powered by steam. Now they are run by electric motors or diesel engines. These are more powerful than steam engines, and can reach full speed much faster. Engineers are still looking for ways to speed up rail travel. In the future, it is likely that trains will be made even faster by using magnets to enable them to float above the track. Trains like this may one day be able to travel as fast as aircraft.

Engineer's cabin

The TGV high-speed train
The TGV or *Train à Grande Vitesse* entered service in 1981, running between Paris and Lyon in France. It can cover 264 miles (425km) in two hours, giving it an average speed of 132mph (212.5km/h).

Overhead electricity
The TGV is powered by electricity at 25,000 volts in an overhead cable. As the train speeds along, it keeps in electrical contact with the cable through an extending arm called a pantograph.

Trains with a difference
Trains do not always run on paired rails. Monorail trains run on a single rail, often high above the ground. Rack-and-pinion trains, which can climb up steep slopes, use three rails. The two outside rails are used for the train's wheels. The extra central rail or rack has teeth on it. The train hauls itself along by gripping these teeth with a powered gear wheel called a pinion. Rack-and-pinion trains are used in mountain areas. In some electric railways, a third rail is used to carry the electricity that powers the trains.

A train without wheels

A maglev train "floats" a tiny distance above the track by using electromagnets. It also uses the electromagnets to push it forward. Because it has no wheels, it produces no friction with the track, and so can travel very quickly and smoothly. The name maglev is short for "magnetic levitation." Maglev trains are still in their experimental stages, and only a few have been built. However, one has already reached speeds of over 310mph (500km/h).

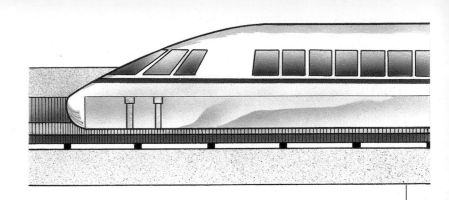

Electric cable

Pantograph

Keeping cool

Air vents in the top of the locomotive let it suck in air to cool the powerful motors.

Providing power

The TGV's electric motors pull eight carriages, containing nearly 400 passengers and their luggage. The train has two power cars – one at each end – and each has a set of motors. The power cars are electronically linked so that their motors turn at the same speed.

Designed for speed

The TGV travels on a track that has been specially designed for high-speed travel. It has smooth slopes and gradual bends. The train is streamlined, and has fewer wheels than an ordinary train of the same size. These features all help it to travel at great speed.

On the tilt

In some experimental high-speed trains, the carriages tilt as the train travels around a corner. This enables the train to corner without having to reduce speed.

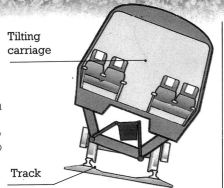

Tilting carriage

Track

DRIVING FORCE

The motor car was invented over 100 years ago. The first "horseless carriages," as they were known, were slow, uncomfortable, and difficult to control. But as the years went by, many ways were found of improving them. The motor age really began in 1908 when the American Henry Ford pioneered the car assembly line. For the first time, cars were cheap enough to be a real alternative to horses.

Today's cars are comfortable, reliable, and efficient in the way they use fuel. Most of them are powered by gasoline. A gasoline engine works by internal combustion, meaning that the fuel is burned in cylinders inside it. This is different from a steam engine, in which the fuel is burned outside.

During this century, more time and money has been spent on developing cars than on any other machines in history. There are already 500 million gasoline-powered vehicles on the roads worldwide, and every year hundreds of new vehicle models are produced. So many cars fill the roads in some countries that it is difficult to travel without becoming stuck in long lines of traffic.

Ready for the road

The car shown here is a rear-wheel drive model, meaning that it is pushed along by its back wheels. Front-wheel drive cars are pulled along by their front wheels. Four-wheel drive cars, which are designed to travel over rough ground, are driven by all their wheels. This car also has a manual gearbox, meaning that the driver has to change gears by using the gear lever. Some cars have automatic gearboxes, which change gear without the driver's help when the engine reaches a certain speed.

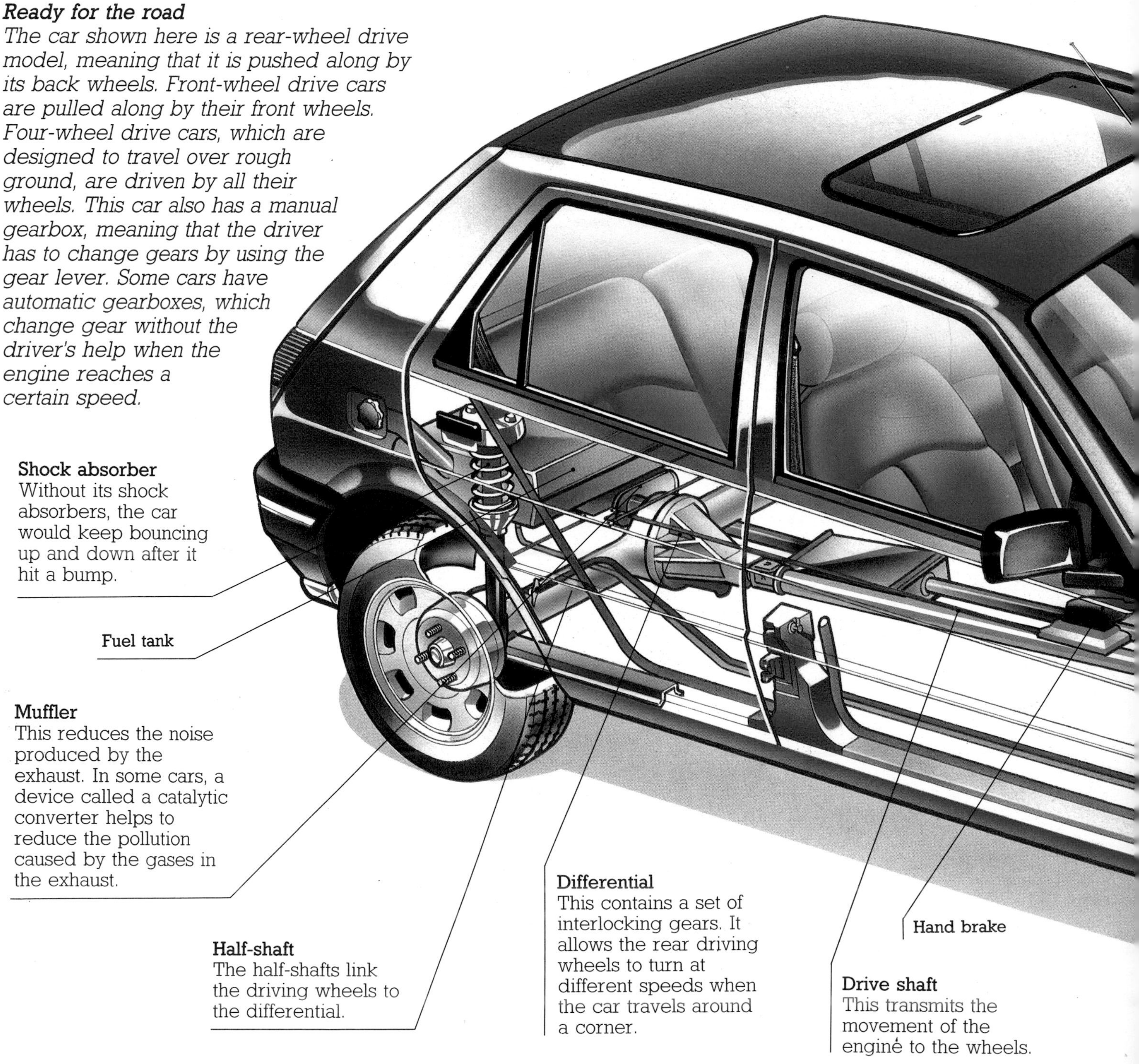

Shock absorber
Without its shock absorbers, the car would keep bouncing up and down after it hit a bump.

Fuel tank

Muffler
This reduces the noise produced by the exhaust. In some cars, a device called a catalytic converter helps to reduce the pollution caused by the gases in the exhaust.

Half-shaft
The half-shafts link the driving wheels to the differential.

Differential
This contains a set of interlocking gears. It allows the rear driving wheels to turn at different speeds when the car travels around a corner.

Hand brake

Drive shaft
This transmits the movement of the engine to the wheels.

The four-stroke engine

A gasoline engine works by producing small explosions inside its cylinders. The carburetor mixes the gasoline and air, and this is sucked into each cylinder in a set order. The mixture is then ignited by a spark plug. The exploding gasoline produces hot gases that force the piston down, and this drives the crankshaft, which turns the wheels. Most car engines run on a four-stroke cycle. This means that the piston moves four times between one explosion and the next.

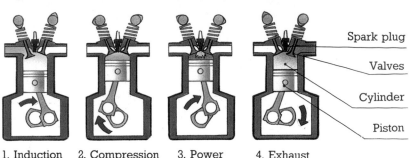

Spark plug
Valves
Cylinder
Piston

1. Induction   2. Compression   3. Power   4. Exhaust

Gear lever

Gears enable the engine to keep running at an efficient speed while the car slows down or speeds up. Most cars have four or five forward gears and one reverse gear.

Steering wheel

The steering wheel is connected to two rods that swivel the front wheels.

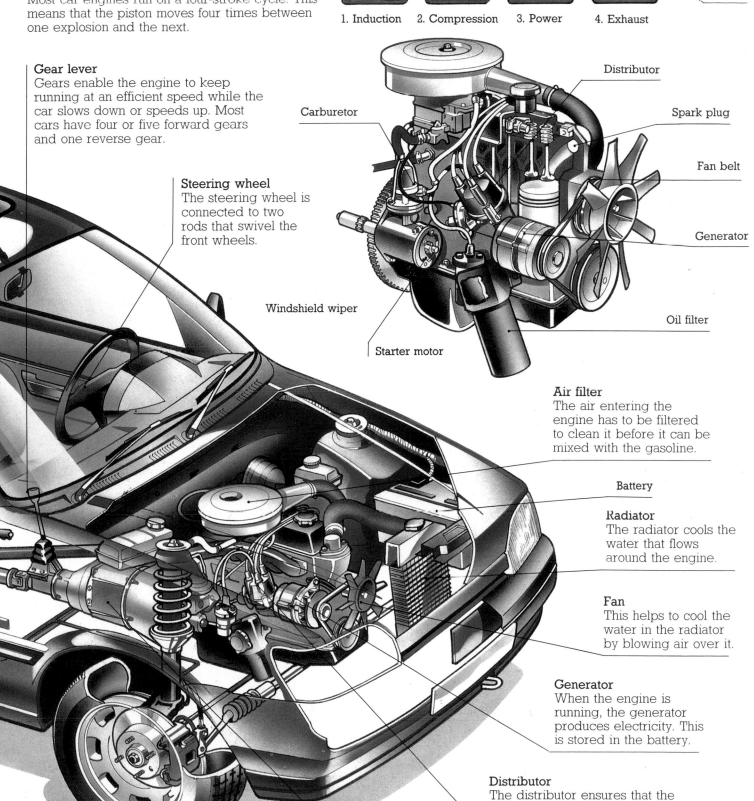

Carburetor

Distributor

Spark plug

Fan belt

Generator

Windshield wiper

Oil filter

Starter motor

Air filter

The air entering the engine has to be filtered to clean it before it can be mixed with the gasoline.

Battery

Radiator

The radiator cools the water that flows around the engine.

Fan

This helps to cool the water in the radiator by blowing air over it.

Generator

When the engine is running, the generator produces electricity. This is stored in the battery.

Distributor

The distributor ensures that the spark plugs fire in a particular order instead of all at once.

Gearbox

MACHINES ON THE MOVE

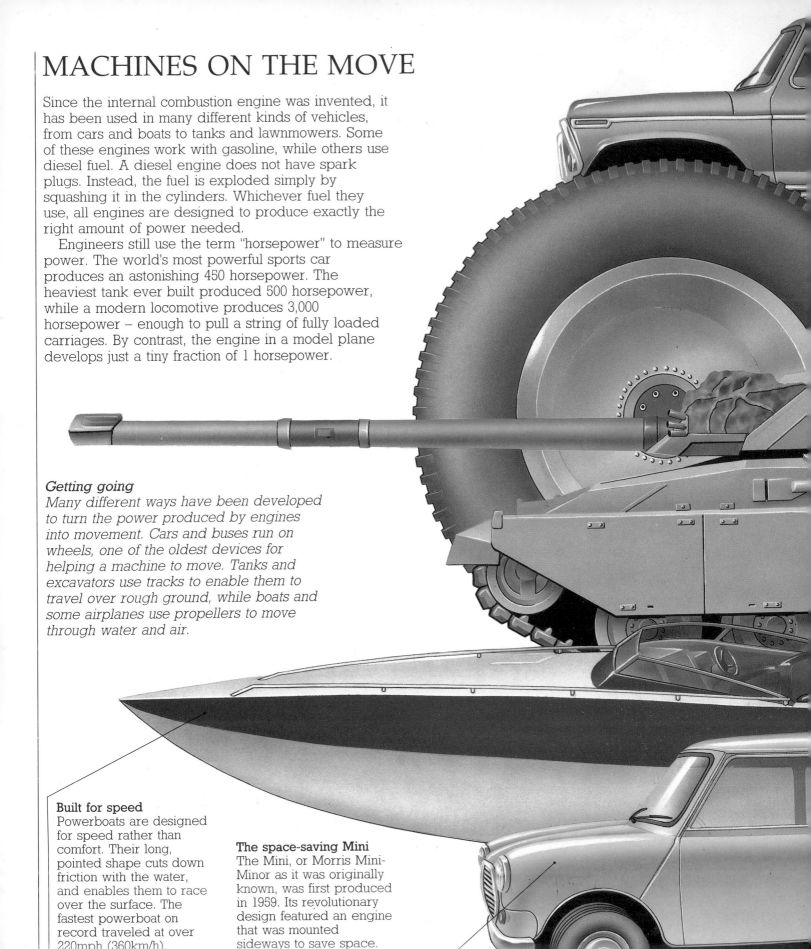

Since the internal combustion engine was invented, it has been used in many different kinds of vehicles, from cars and boats to tanks and lawnmowers. Some of these engines work with gasoline, while others use diesel fuel. A diesel engine does not have spark plugs. Instead, the fuel is exploded simply by squashing it in the cylinders. Whichever fuel they use, all engines are designed to produce exactly the right amount of power needed.

Engineers still use the term "horsepower" to measure power. The world's most powerful sports car produces an astonishing 450 horsepower. The heaviest tank ever built produced 500 horsepower, while a modern locomotive produces 3,000 horsepower – enough to pull a string of fully loaded carriages. By contrast, the engine in a model plane develops just a tiny fraction of 1 horsepower.

Getting going
Many different ways have been developed to turn the power produced by engines into movement. Cars and buses run on wheels, one of the oldest devices for helping a machine to move. Tanks and excavators use tracks to enable them to travel over rough ground, while boats and some airplanes use propellers to move through water and air.

Built for speed
Powerboats are designed for speed rather than comfort. Their long, pointed shape cuts down friction with the water, and enables them to race over the surface. The fastest powerboat on record traveled at over 220mph (360km/h).

The space-saving Mini
The Mini, or Morris Mini-Minor as it was originally known, was first produced in 1959. Its revolutionary design featured an engine that was mounted sideways to save space. Today, many small cars have "transverse" engines like the Mini.

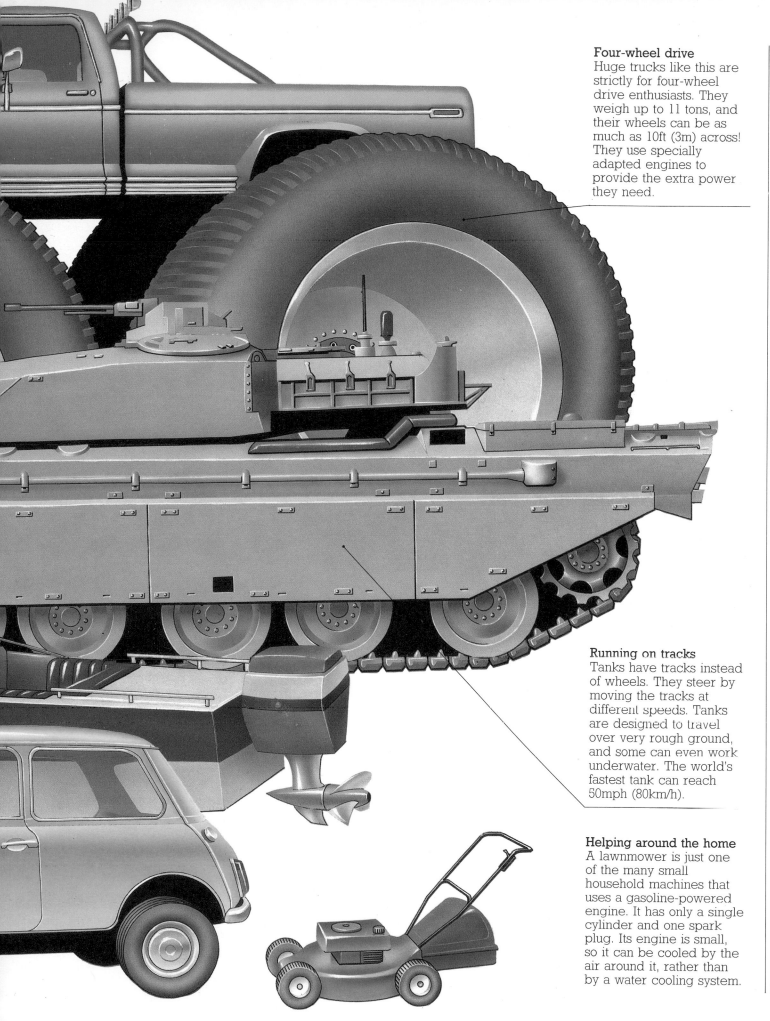

Four-wheel drive
Huge trucks like this are strictly for four-wheel drive enthusiasts. They weigh up to 11 tons, and their wheels can be as much as 10ft (3m) across! They use specially adapted engines to provide the extra power they need.

Running on tracks
Tanks have tracks instead of wheels. They steer by moving the tracks at different speeds. Tanks are designed to travel over very rough ground, and some can even work underwater. The world's fastest tank can reach 50mph (80km/h).

Helping around the home
A lawnmower is just one of the many small household machines that uses a gasoline-powered engine. It has only a single cylinder and one spark plug. Its engine is small, so it can be cooled by the air around it, rather than by a water cooling system.

FLOATING ON AIR

If you have ever been on a boat, you will know that traveling over water is usually a slow business. This is because water is much denser than air, and it gets in the way of anything trying to move through it. This effect is called water resistance. The bigger a boat is, the more area it has in contact with the water, and the more water resistance it has to overcome.

However, two kinds of transport – Hovercraft and hydrofoils - can travel much faster than boats. This is because much less of them is in contact with the water. A Hovercraft is like a cross between a boat and a plane. Instead of floating, it flies just above the surface of the water on a cushion of air. Only the edge of its inflatable skirt actually touches the water. A hydrofoil skims across the water on small fins that lift its hull clear of the surface. The fastest Hovercraft can reach speeds of 65 knots (75mph), while the fastest hydrofoils can travel at about 50 knots (56mph).

Giant Hovercraft
The Class SRN4 MkIII is the world's largest passenger-carrying Hovercraft. It is over 180 feet (55m) long and weight over 273 tons. These giant craft cross the English Channel in a fraction of the time taken by an ordinary ferry.

How a Hovercraft works
In a Class SRN4 MkIII Hovercraft, air is pumped into the inflatable skirt by four fans housed just beneath the upper deck. These provide the lift that keeps the Hovercraft above the water. The propellers are similar to those in a plane, except that they push the Hovercraft forward rather than pulling it along.

Loading door
Cars drive onto the Hovercraft through the loading door at the front, and leave it through the disembarkation doors at the rear. A Class SRN4 MkIII Hovercraft can carry up to 60 cars and over 400 passengers.

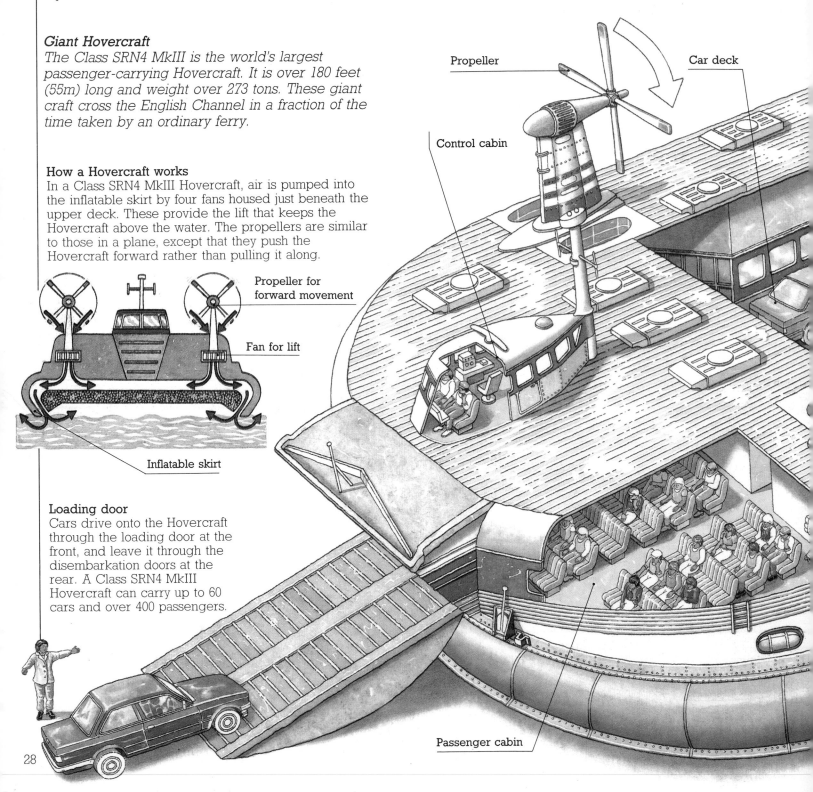

Propeller

Car deck

Control cabin

Propeller for forward movement

Fan for lift

Inflatable skirt

Passenger cabin

28

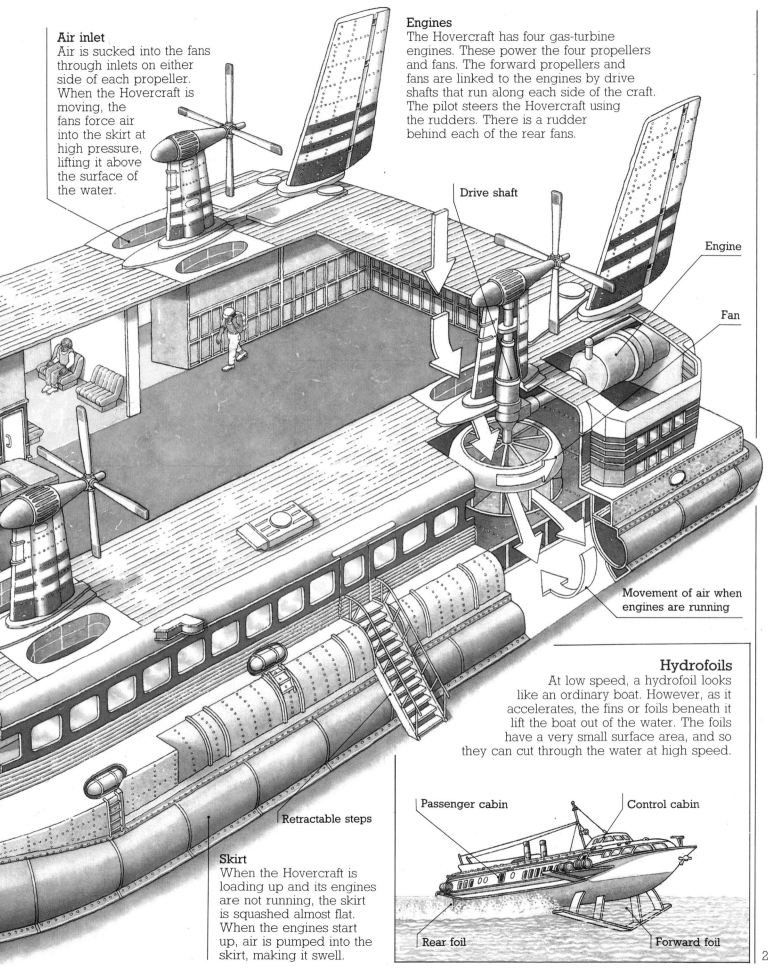

Air inlet
Air is sucked into the fans through inlets on either side of each propeller. When the Hovercraft is moving, the fans force air into the skirt at high pressure, lifting it above the surface of the water.

Engines
The Hovercraft has four gas-turbine engines. These power the four propellers and fans. The forward propellers and fans are linked to the engines by drive shafts that run along each side of the craft. The pilot steers the Hovercraft using the rudders. There is a rudder behind each of the rear fans.

Drive shaft

Engine

Fan

Movement of air when engines are running

Retractable steps

Skirt
When the Hovercraft is loading up and its engines are not running, the skirt is squashed almost flat. When the engines start up, air is pumped into the skirt, making it swell.

Hydrofoils
At low speed, a hydrofoil looks like an ordinary boat. However, as it accelerates, the fins or foils beneath it lift the boat out of the water. The foils have a very small surface area, and so they can cut through the water at high speed.

Passenger cabin

Control cabin

Rear foil

Forward foil

UNDER PRESSURE

Mechanical diggers and pneumatic drills are two kinds of machines that work by pressure. A digger is an example of a hydraulic machine. It uses its engine to squeeze hydraulic fluid until it is at many times the pressure of the atmosphere. This fluid is then used to power a set of rams that operates the digger. Each ram consists of a cylinder and a sliding piston. When the driver operates one of the rams, a valve opens and the fluid enters the cylinder. The fluid pushes the piston outward with great force, moving the digger's arm or tilting its bucket. Hydraulic power is used in many machines, from car jacks to giant presses.

Pneumatic machines work with air instead of a fluid. The air is squeezed by a compressor. When the machine is used, air flows from the compressor into a cylinder, where it pushes a piston. Pneumatic power is used in devices such as automatic doors and air brakes.

An artificial arm
Although it can only move up and down, the excavating arm of a mechanical digger is otherwise very much like a human arm.

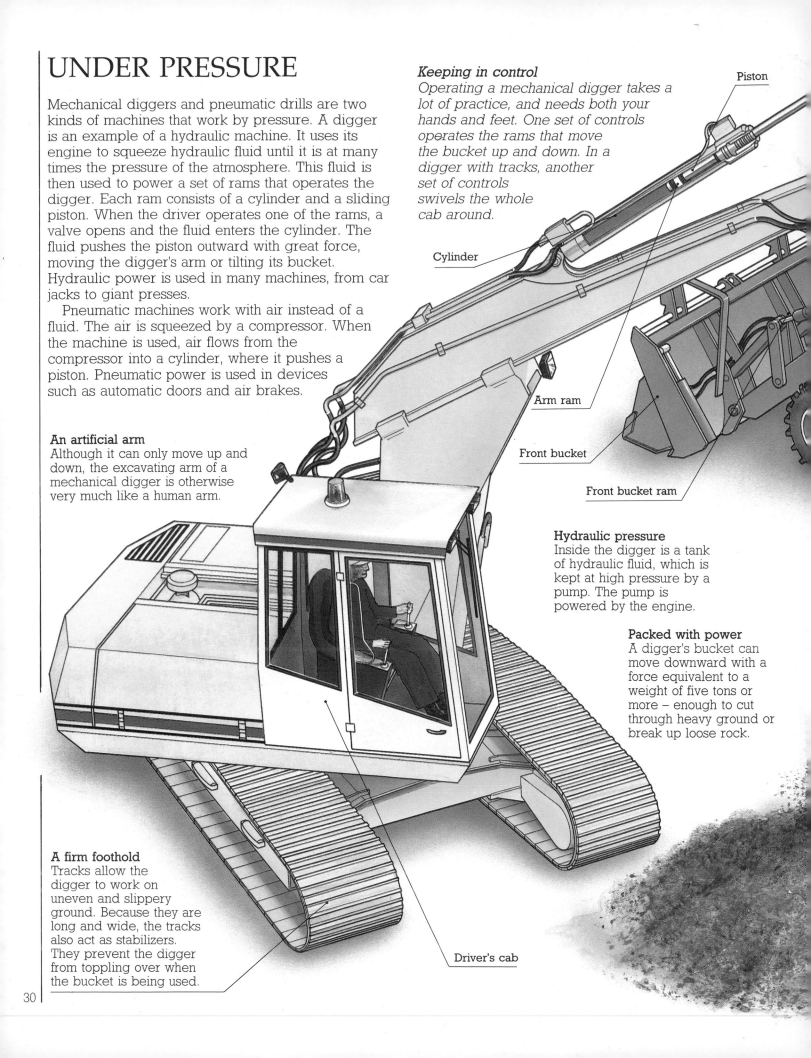

Keeping in control
Operating a mechanical digger takes a lot of practice, and needs both your hands and feet. One set of controls operates the rams that move the bucket up and down. In a digger with tracks, another set of controls swivels the whole cab around.

Piston

Cylinder

Arm ram

Front bucket

Front bucket ram

Hydraulic pressure
Inside the digger is a tank of hydraulic fluid, which is kept at high pressure by a pump. The pump is powered by the engine.

Packed with power
A digger's bucket can move downward with a force equivalent to a weight of five tons or more – enough to cut through heavy ground or break up loose rock.

A firm foothold
Tracks allow the digger to work on uneven and slippery ground. Because they are long and wide, the tracks also act as stabilizers. They prevent the digger from toppling over when the bucket is being used.

Driver's cab

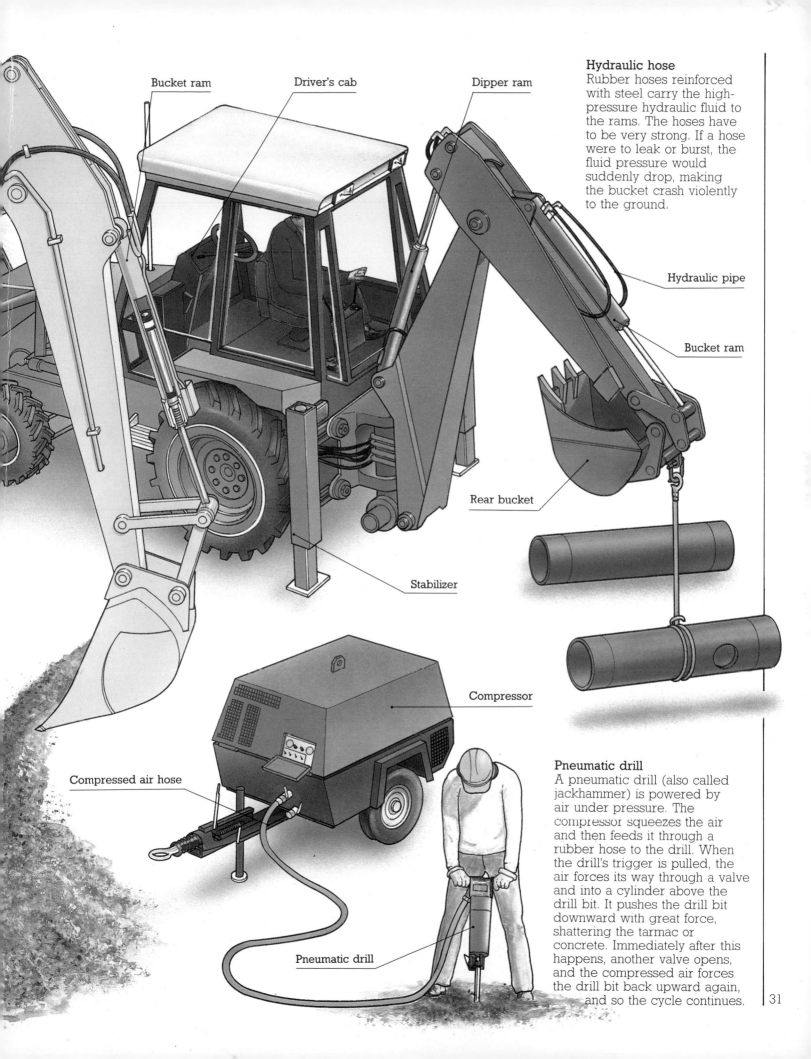

Bucket ram

Driver's cab

Dipper ram

Hydraulic hose
Rubber hoses reinforced with steel carry the high-pressure hydraulic fluid to the rams. The hoses have to be very strong. If a hose were to leak or burst, the fluid pressure would suddenly drop, making the bucket crash violently to the ground.

Hydraulic pipe

Bucket ram

Rear bucket

Stabilizer

Compressor

Compressed air hose

Pneumatic drill

Pneumatic drill
A pneumatic drill (also called jackhammer) is powered by air under pressure. The compressor squeezes the air and then feeds it through a rubber hose to the drill. When the drill's trigger is pulled, the air forces its way through a valve and into a cylinder above the drill bit. It pushes the drill bit downward with great force, shattering the tarmac or concrete. Immediately after this happens, another valve opens, and the compressed air forces the drill bit back upward again, and so the cycle continues.

BUILDING WITH CONCRETE

If you watch a modern office block being built, you may be surprised to see how fast it goes up once the foundations have been laid. First, a steel frame is bolted together, and then, as the frame increases in size, it is filled with concrete floors and walls. The concrete is not normally made up on the building site. Instead, it is brought in by a fleet of mixers that then unload it into a special mobile pump.

A large mixer truck has a continuously rotating barrel that holds up to 16.5 tons of concrete. Inside the barrel are curved metal blades. As the barrel turns, these churn up the concrete, keeping it well mixed and helping to prevent it from setting. When the mixer arrives at the building site, the concrete is unloaded into the mobile pump. This has a powerful piston that forces the concrete up and into the building.

A two-machine team

Working together, a mixer and pump can unload 16.5 tons of concrete in the space of a few minutes. Both machines have to work quickly, because the concrete must be pumped into position while it is still liquid enough to spread easily. The concrete travels down the mixer's unloading channel and into the pump's loading hopper. From here, it flows into the pump and up the pipe.

Unloading the concrete

When the mixer arrives at the building site, the driver unfolds the unloading channel. To unload the concrete, the driver switches over the mixer barrel so that it turns in reverse. The blades inside the barrel force the concrete upward until it pours out through the unloading channel into the concrete pump.

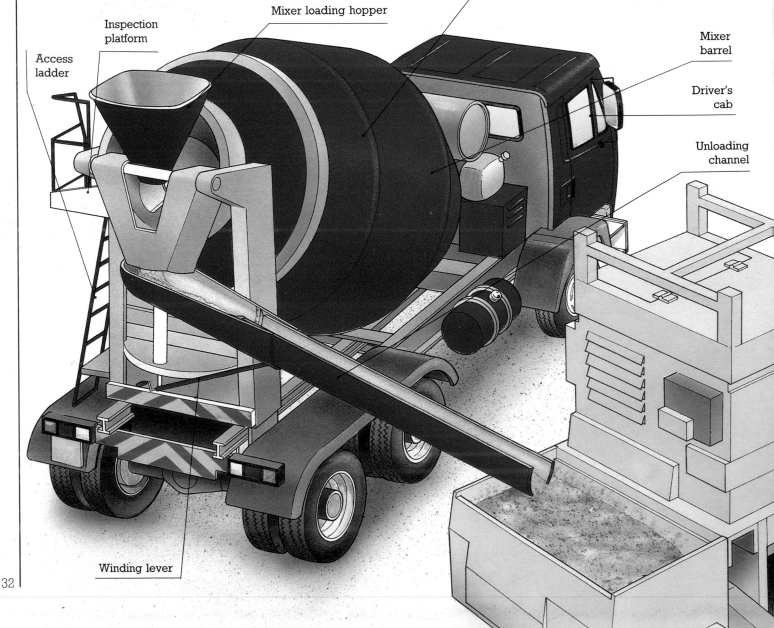

Access ladder

Inspection platform

Mixer loading hopper

Mixer barrel

Driver's cab

Unloading channel

Winding lever

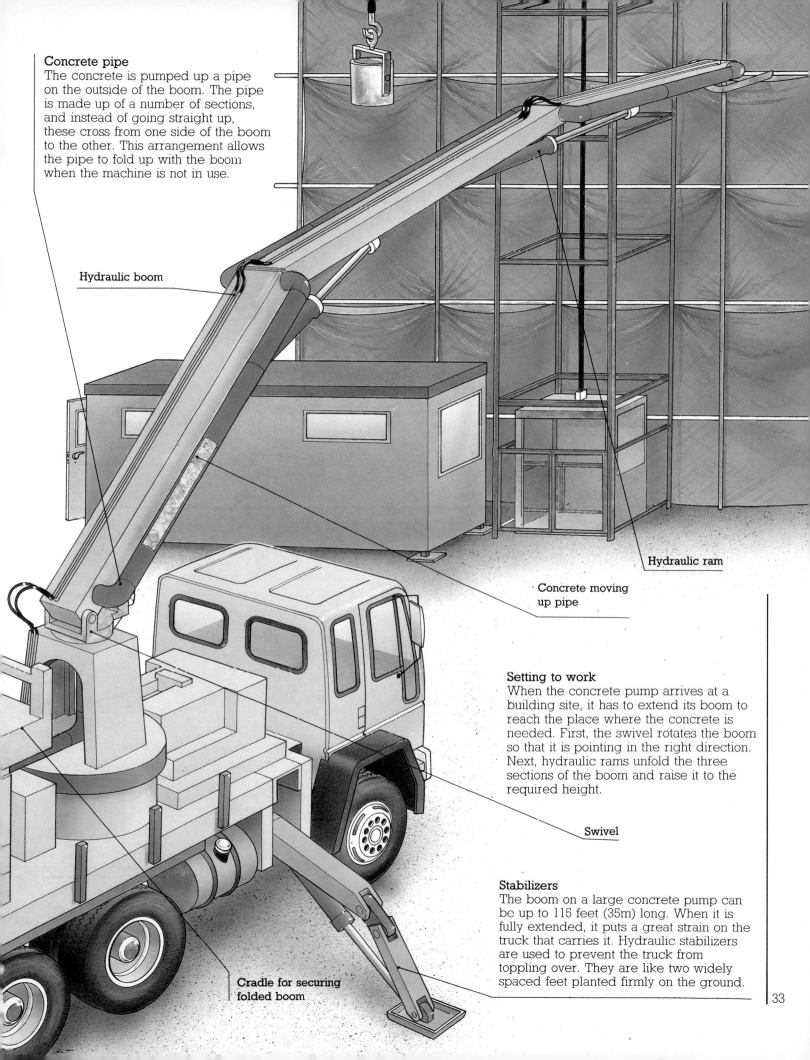

Concrete pipe
The concrete is pumped up a pipe on the outside of the boom. The pipe is made up of a number of sections, and instead of going straight up, these cross from one side of the boom to the other. This arrangement allows the pipe to fold up with the boom when the machine is not in use.

Hydraulic boom

Hydraulic ram

Concrete moving up pipe

Setting to work
When the concrete pump arrives at a building site, it has to extend its boom to reach the place where the concrete is needed. First, the swivel rotates the boom so that it is pointing in the right direction. Next, hydraulic rams unfold the three sections of the boom and raise it to the required height.

Swivel

Stabilizers
The boom on a large concrete pump can be up to 115 feet (35m) long. When it is fully extended, it puts a great strain on the truck that carries it. Hydraulic stabilizers are used to prevent the truck from toppling over. They are like two widely spaced feet planted firmly on the ground.

Cradle for securing folded boom

TAKING THE STRAIN

Tower cranes are used on construction sites to build high-rise apartments and office buildings. Instead of carrying materials over the ground, a tower crane lifts them through the air, lowering them with pin-point accuracy. It has a long jib that swings around and a counterweight to balance the loads it lifts.

A tower crane arrives at a building site in separate pieces. First, the bottom section of the tower is fixed onto a concrete base; then the tower is bolted together in sections until it reaches the required height. In some cranes, the sections are assembled using a mobile crane. In others, the crane builds itself with a special hydraulic system that lifts the jib upward.

Pulley power
Tower cranes are operated by electric motors connected to winches. The winches wind in strong steel cables that are looped around a number of pulleys. Cranes use pulleys to make the work easier for their motors. Pulleys reduce the force that the motors have to exert to raise the load. In return for this, they increase the amount of cable that has to be wound in.

Main jib

The cab
The crane driver sits in a cab just below the jib. Controls in the cab operate electric motors that hoist the trolley and its pulleys. From so far up, it is difficult for the driver to see exactly what is happening below. A worker on the ground guides the driver using a walkie-talkie.

Hook

Alarm system
The strain on the jib is greatest when the trolley is at the far end of the jib. The weight acts like someone pulling on a very long lever. An alarm system in the cabin lets the crane driver know if the weight is too heavy for the crane to lift.

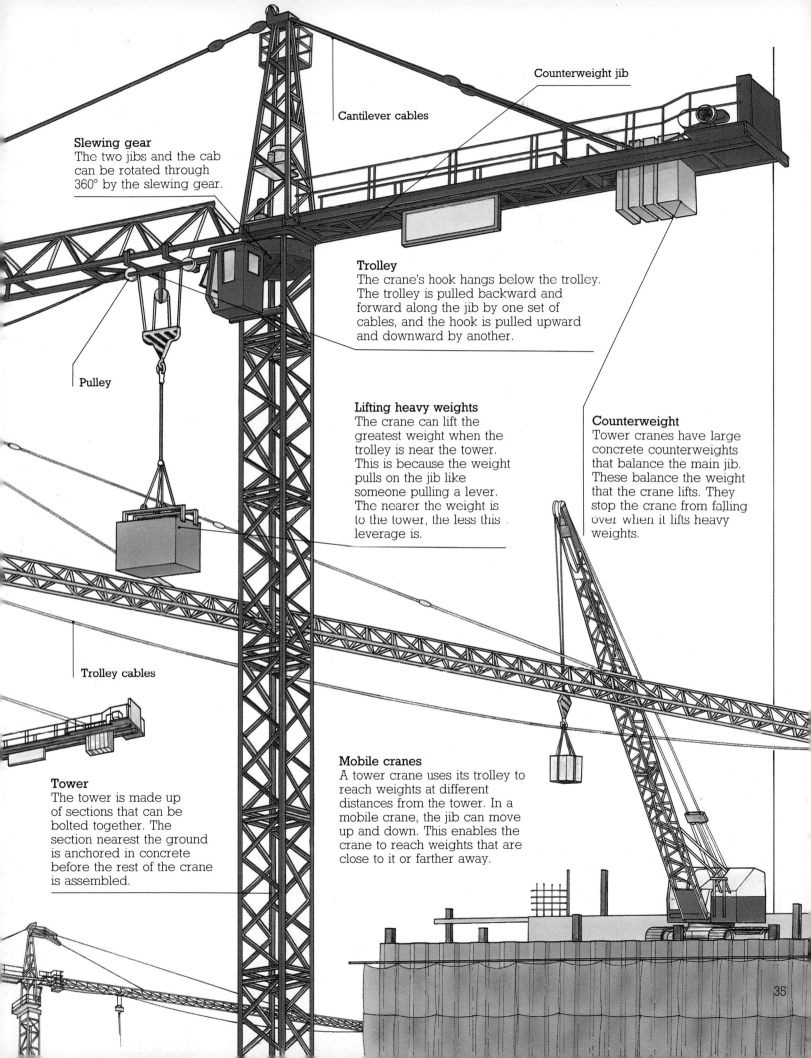

Counterweight jib

Cantilever cables

Slewing gear
The two jibs and the cab
can be rotated through
360° by the slewing gear.

Trolley
The crane's hook hangs below the trolley.
The trolley is pulled backward and
forward along the jib by one set of
cables, and the hook is pulled upward
and downward by another.

Pulley

Lifting heavy weights
The crane can lift the
greatest weight when the
trolley is near the tower.
This is because the weight
pulls on the jib like
someone pulling a lever.
The nearer the weight is
to the tower, the less this
leverage is.

Counterweight
Tower cranes have large
concrete counterweights
that balance the main jib.
These balance the weight
that the crane lifts. They
stop the crane from falling
over when it lifts heavy
weights.

Trolley cables

Tower
The tower is made up
of sections that can be
bolted together. The
section nearest the ground
is anchored in concrete
before the rest of the crane
is assembled.

Mobile cranes
A tower crane uses its trolley to
reach weights at different
distances from the tower. In a
mobile crane, the jib can move
up and down. This enables the
crane to reach weights that are
close to it or farther away.

35

MADE TO MEASURE

At one time, the human body was the only measuring device available. Length was measured in paces or arms, or even fingers. Then machines and devices were invented specially for measuring. Rulers and tape measures give the size of large objects, while micrometers tell us the size of small ones. We use scales to measure weight, and speedometers to find out how fast something is traveling.

Many different instruments are used to tell us about the weather. The two most important are the thermometer and the barometer. A thermometer tells us how hot it is, by measuring the expansion of a liquid, such as mercury or alcohol, as it gets warm. The hotter it is, the more the liquid expands. A

Maximum and minimum thermometer

A maximum and minimum thermometer contains mercury and alcohol. When it gets cold, the mercury rises up the left-hand side of the tube, pushing a metal marker upward. When it gets warmer again, the mercury falls in the left-hand side, leaving the marker in position, and rises on the right, again pushing a marker upward. The markers show how hot and cold it has been. To reset the markers, they are pulled downward using a magnet.

Aneroid barometer

An aneroid barometer uses a flattened metal drum to register changes in air pressure. The drum contains a vacuum, and its sides are held apart by a spring. The sides come closer together when the air pressure rises, and move farther apart when it falls. A system of levers, wires, and springs carries this movement from the drum to the pointer. The word aneroid means "no air" – referring to the vacuum inside the drum.

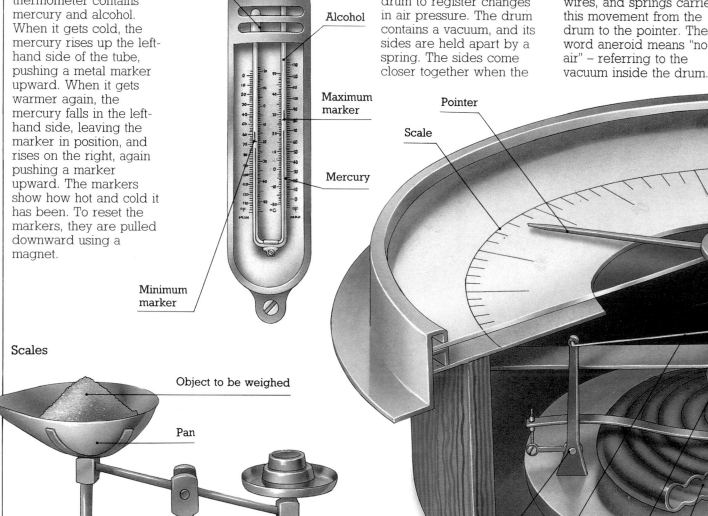

Air

Alcohol

Maximum marker

Mercury

Minimum marker

Pointer

Scale

Lever

Wire

Spring

Vacuum inside drum

Scales

Object to be weighed

Pan

Weights

Weighing scales, or balances, are among the oldest measuring machines. To weigh an object, you place it on the left-hand pan. You then add weights to the right-hand pan until the pans just balance. Adding up the value of the weights then gives you the weight of the object. Today, spring-operated scales are more common than ones that use weights. In these, the object to be weighed stretches a spring, moving a pointer or dial.

barometer tells us how great the air pressure is. It does this either by measuring how far the atmosphere can push against a sprung metal drum, or by how much mercury it can support in a closed tube. When the pressure is high, the weather is usually settled and dry. If the pressure is low, there may be a spell of wet and stormy weather.

Fortin barometer
With this kind of barometer, the air pressure is measured by the height of a column of mercury inside a glass tube. The top of the tube is sealed, and contains a vacuum.

Scale

Mercury in glass tube

Case

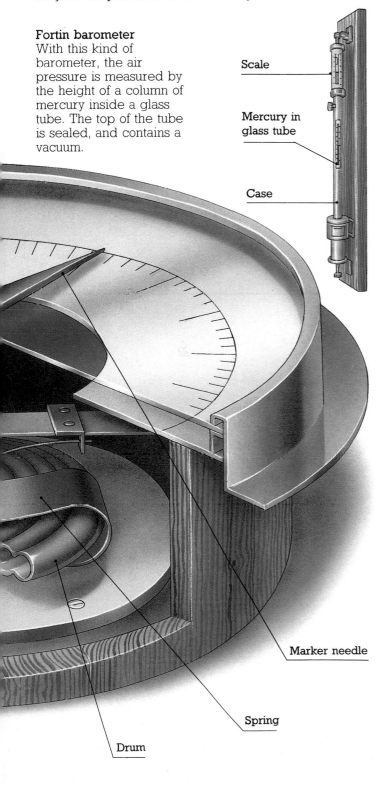

Marker needle

Spring

Drum

Choose your units
To measure anything, we need a system of units. Today, many countries have adopted the metric system, which uses meters, kilograms, and liters. Other countries use the imperial system, with units that include feet, pounds, and gallons.

Speedometer

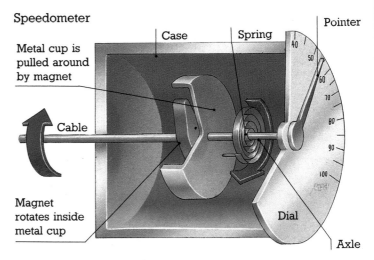

Metal cup is pulled around by magnet

Case

Spring

Pointer

Cable

40
50
60
70
80
90
100

Magnet rotates inside metal cup

Dial

Axle

A car's speedometer is operated by a cable that is rotated by the engine. The cable turns a magnet that is surrounded by a metal cup. The cup tries to follow the magnet, and it turns an axle connected to the pointer. The faster the cable rotates, the farther the cup turns and the more the pointer moves. A spring makes sure that the position of the pointer is proportional to the movement of the magnet.

Micrometer
A micrometer is used to measure the width of small objects very precisely. The object is placed between the spindle and anvil, and the barrel is wound toward the anvil until the object is held tight. Its width can then be read from two scales marked on the barrel.

Barrel

Scale

Scale

Spindle

Anvil

Object being measured

SUCTION MACHINES

Although we cannot feel it, the atmosphere above us is very heavy. The weight of air that presses down on a small table, for example, is about 5 tons. The only reason the table does not collapse is that the atmosphere presses against all its surfaces – underneath as well as on top. Suction machines such as the vacuum cleaner put the pressure of the atmosphere to work. They blow the air out of a closed space so that the pressure of the atmosphere forces more air in to take its place. In the vacuum cleaner, the incoming air carries dust and dirt with it.

Cylinder vacuum cleaner

In this kind of vaccum cleaner, the fan lies behind the dust bag. It blows air out of the back of the cleaner, and so air and dust flow in up the hose. The incoming air can escape through the bag, but the dust is trapped inside it.

Drinking through a straw

When you suck through a straw, the pressure in your mouth becomes less than that of the air outside. The pressure of the air on the drink then forces the liquid up the straw and into your mouth.

Liquid moves up straw

Trapping the dust

When the vacuum cleaner is turned on, the bag swells up as air is sucked into it. The bag is made of a material that air can travel through. Dust particles are too big to pass through the bag and so they collect inside it.

Power source

Dust left behind

Incoming air

Hose

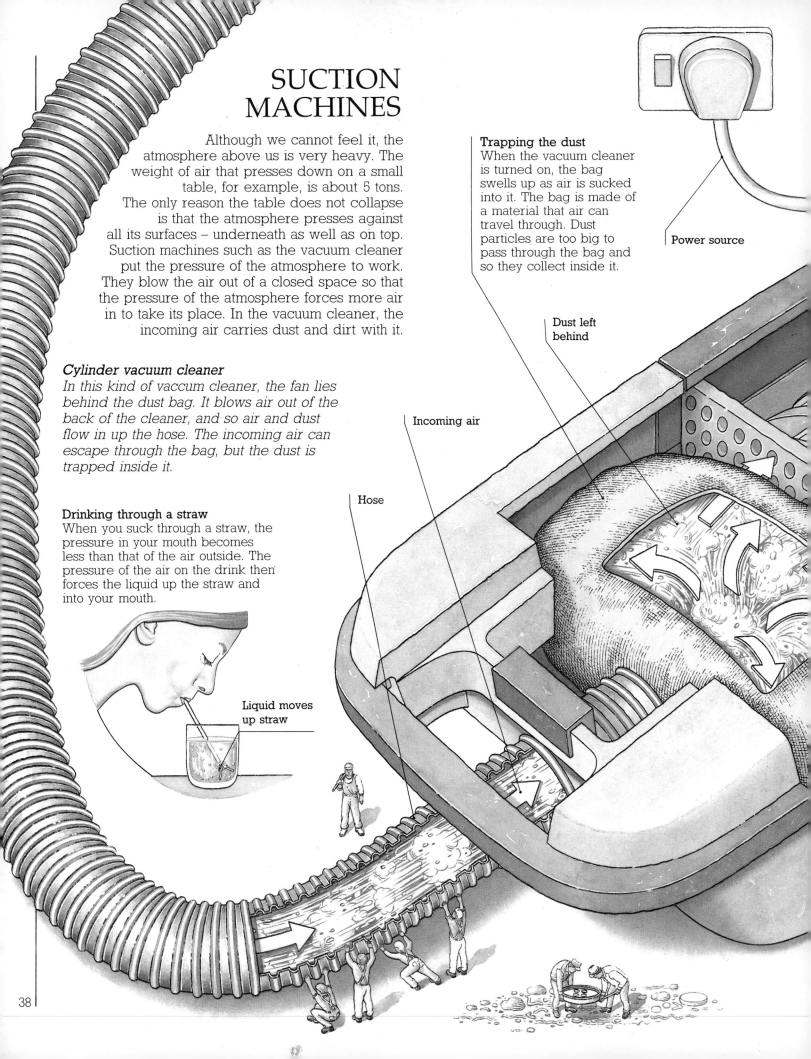

Switch on/off

Blowing air out
The blades of the fan turn at high speed, blowing air out of the rear part of the cleaner. This reduces the air pressure inside the cleaner, so that more air rushes in through the bag.

Outgoing air

Motor

Nozzle
The vacuum cleaner has specially shaped brushes and nozzles that fit on the end of the hose. Air rushes through the brush or nozzle and into the hose, pulling dust with it.

Upright vacuum cleaners
The first vacuum cleaner was invented by Hubert Booth in 1901. It was powered by a gasoline engine, and was so big and heavy that it had to be mounted on a cart and pulled by a horse. The upright vacuum cleaner was invented by Murray Spangler and marketed by W. Hoover a year later. Spangler's vacuum cleaner was powered not by gasoline but by a small electric motor, making it suitable for use in the home. The design was so successful that millions of upright vacuum cleaners have since been made. An upright vacuum cleaner works in a slightly different way from a cylinder cleaner. The fan is in front of the dust bag instead of behind it. The air and dust travel through the blades of the fan and are blown into the bag. This kind of vacuum cleaner also beats and brushes carpets to dislodge dust.

Dust bag

Hose

Motor

Fan

Dust

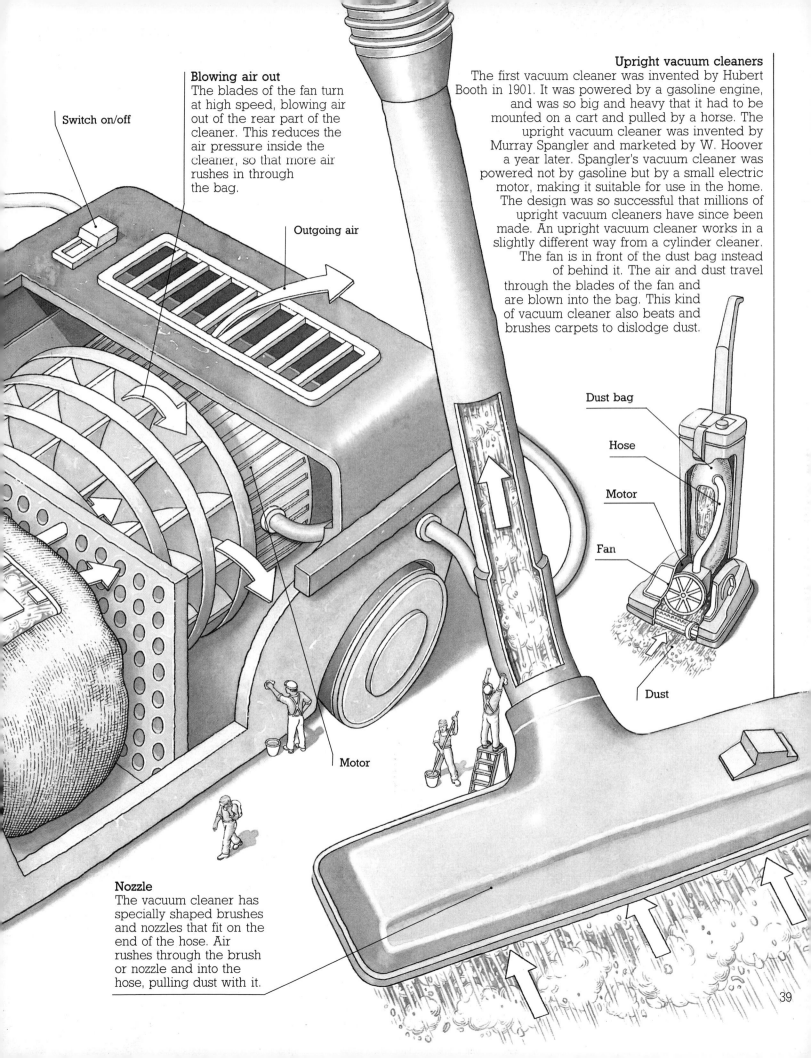

IN A WHIRL

What happens if you tie a weight to the end of a piece of string and whirl it around? The answer is easy – the weight travels in a circle, and the string is pulled tight. But what happens if you are whirling the weight and the string suddenly breaks? The weight will fly off into the air. Instead of staying on its circular path, it will travel in a straight path over the ground.

This shows that anything moving in a circle is always trying to carry on in a straight line. To keep something moving in a circle, you need to apply a force to it. This force is called "centripetal force." Centripetal force keeps the weight on a circular path and makes the string tight. It is the same force that keeps satellites in orbit, and that pushes you in a curve when a car turns a corner.

Machines such as the spin drier and roller coaster both make use of movement in a circle. The roller coaster uses it to keep you in your seat, while the spin drier uses it to force water out of wet clothes.

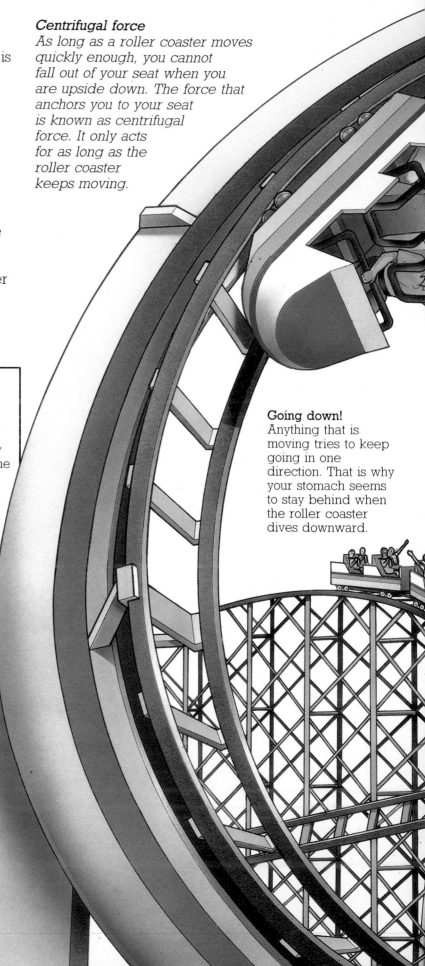

Centrifugal force
As long as a roller coaster moves quickly enough, you cannot fall out of your seat when you are upside down. The force that anchors you to your seat is known as centrifugal force. It only acts for as long as the roller coaster keeps moving.

Going down!
Anything that is moving tries to keep going in one direction. That is why your stomach seems to stay behind when the roller coaster dives downward.

Spin drier
To use a spin drier, the wet clothes are put inside the drum. When the lid is closed, the drum starts to rotate. It speeds up, eventually spinning thousands of times every minute. The clothes are thrown outward but they keep moving in a circle because they are held in by the drum. However, the water in them is able to flow out through the holes in the drum. It runs down between the drum and the case, and out of a spout. Some spin driers have a pump that collects the water and forces it out through a pipe.

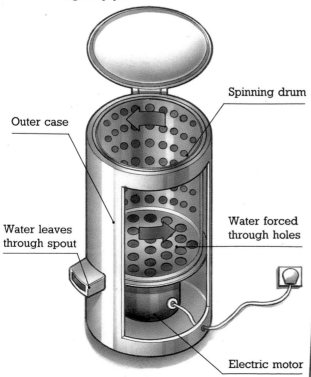

Spinning drum

Outer case

Water leaves
through spout

Water forced
through holes

Electric motor

Putting on weight
As the roller coaster speeds upward, the acceleration against the pull of gravity makes you feel heavier than you are on the ground.

Locked in position
The wheels of roller coaster cars are locked into grooves on their rails. If they were not anchored in this way, the cars would fly into the air when traveling on the outside of steep curves.

Fixed to the seat
When the roller coaster is upside down, your body tries to move horizontally forward. It cannot do this, because the seat is in the way and holds you in.

Getting going
Many roller coasters are powered by gravity. The cars are pulled up to the top of a steep slope and then released. Gravity gives them enough speed to hurtle on a hair-raising ride through all the track's twists and turns. Some roller coasters are powered by cables that run between the two rails.

KEEPING COOL

Refrigerators and boilers are two machines that work by transferring heat from one place to another. A refrigerator is used to remove heat from something, while a boiler is used to produce it.

To understand how a refrigerator works, you can try a simple experiment. Next time you go for a swim, stand still for a few minutes as soon as you get out of the water. You will start to feel quite cold, even if the air around you is warm. This is because the water on your body will start to turn into water vapor. To do this, it needs a great deal of heat energy. It gets this heat from your body, and so your skin becomes cold.

A refrigerator works in a similar way. It uses the warmth of food to help turn a special liquid, called a refrigerant, into a vapor. As the vapor is formed, the food cools down. The vapor is then pumped into a long tube behind the refrigerator, where it condenses, or becomes a liquid once again. As it does this, it gives up warmth it collected from the food.

Cooling liquids
To keep food cool, refrigerators use special liquids that turn into a vapor at low temperatures. Most refrigerators use liquids called CFCs, which is short for "chlorofluorocarbons."

Condenser
The condenser is a long curved pipe attached to rows of metal rods. As the refrigerant is pumped through the pipe, it condenses or turns into a liquid, giving out the heat it collected from the food.

Freezer
A refrigerator keeps food at temperatures between 34°F (1°C) and 39°F (4°C). A freezer keeps food much colder: between 0°F (−18°C) and −31°F (−35°C). This means that certain foods can be kept in a freezer for several months.

Compressor
The compressor is a small electric motor that drives the refrigerant in a circle from condenser to the freezer and back again. It is controlled by a thermostat. When the temperature inside the refrigerator rises, this causes the thermostat to turn the compressor on. Once the refrigerator has cooled down, the compressor is switched off.

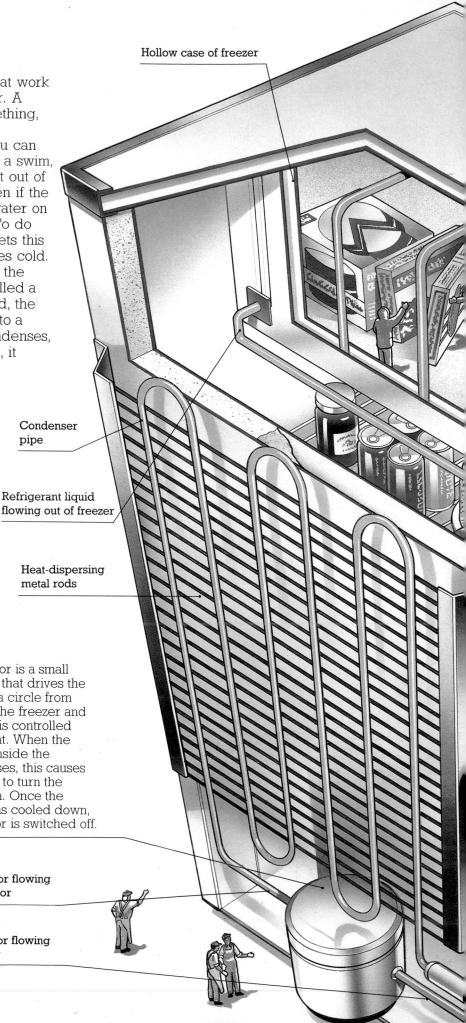

Hollow case of freezer

Condenser pipe

Refrigerant liquid flowing out of freezer

Heat-dispersing metal rods

Refrigerant vapor flowing out of compressor

Refrigerant vapor flowing into compressor

42

Refrigerant vapor
flowing into freezer

Boiler

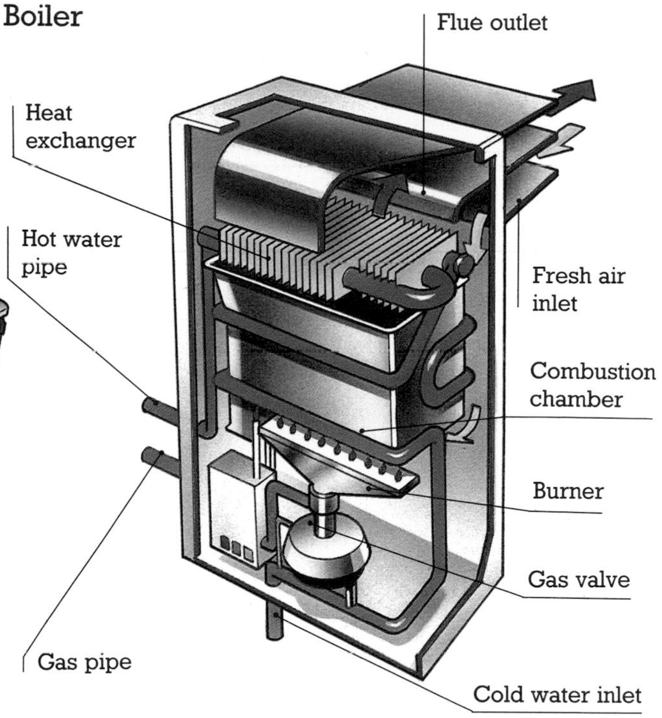

Flue outlet

Heat
exchanger

Hot water
pipe

Fresh air
inlet

Combustion
chamber

Burner

Gas valve

Gas pipe

Cold water inlet

In a boiler, a fuel or electricity is used to supply the heat needed to warm up water. Boilers are designed so that as much energy as possible is turned into useful heat. To do this, they use a heat exchanger – a device that acts much like a radiator in reverse. Instead of giving out heat, the heat exchanger collects it and uses it to warm the water. The boiler shown here is fueled by gas. It is activated whenever a hot-water tap is turned on.

Freezer compartment

The motor pumps the refrigerant liquid through a pipe to the freezer compartment. When it reaches the freezer it is forced through a narrow valve. This makes the liquid turn into a vapor, which then flows through the freezer's hollow lining. When the liquid turns into a vapor, it takes in a lot of heat. This heat comes from the food, making it so cold that it freezes.

Narrow valve
in pipe

Insulated casing

A refrigerator has a special casing that stops the warmth of the air outside reaching the food inside. The outside of the fridge is made of a thin sheet of metal, while the inner lining is made of a hard plastic. Between the two is a thick layer of an insulator, such as expanded polystyrene. This acts as a barrier to warmth from outside.

FIGHTING FIRE

In order to burn, a fire has to have oxygen. If you throw water on a fire, it will go out. This is because the water prevents the oxygen in the air from reaching the fuel. The machines that are used to fight fires all make use of this principle. Fire extinguishers cut off the supply of oxygen in a number of different ways. Some use water, while others use heavy gases, such as carbon dioxide. These gases push aside the air that surrounds an object on fire so that the flames die out. Extinguishers can put a stop to small fires, but if a fire has already spread out of control, bigger machines have to be called in. Fire trucks and turntable ladders are used to bring large fires under control and rescue anyone trapped by the flames. In an airport, a special kind of fire truck called a crash tender is used. This is specially designed to race across the tarmac to the scene of an accident. Its powerful pump sprays foam over the stricken aircraft, dousing the flames and keeping oxygen away from the plane's highly inflammable fuel.

High-rise rescue
Turntable ladders and hydraulic platforms allow fire fighters to rescue people and fight fires high above the gound. The longest turntable ladders reach a height of 160 feet (50m) when they are fully extended – enough to reach to the twelfth floor of a high-rise building.

Going up
The ladder is made up of a number of separate sections, and is fitted with two sets of steel cables. These are wound by electric winches. One set is used to make the ladder extend, while the other set makes it retract.

Fire hydrant

Quenching the flames
Some rescue ladders have a built-in water hose that can be used to tackle fires high up. The hose is controlled either by a fire fighter on the ladder, or if this is too dangerous, by a remote-control panel on the ground.

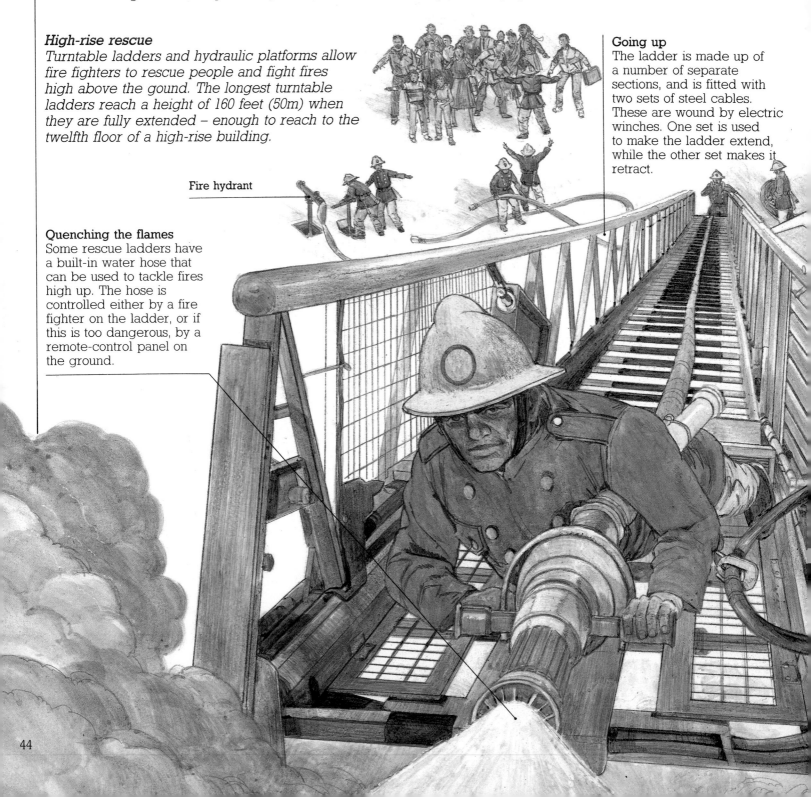

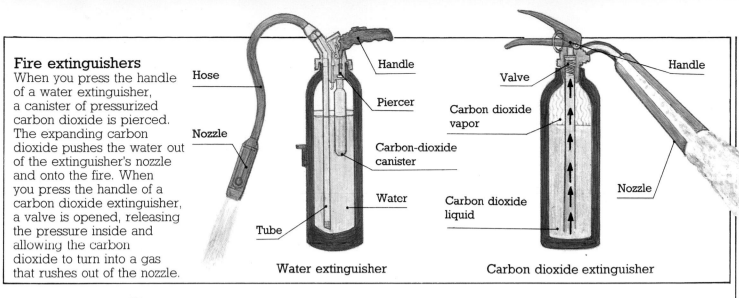

Fire extinguishers

When you press the handle of a water extinguisher, a canister of pressurized carbon dioxide is pierced. The expanding carbon dioxide pushes the water out of the extinguisher's nozzle and onto the fire. When you press the handle of a carbon dioxide extinguisher, a valve is opened, releasing the pressure inside and allowing the carbon dioxide to turn into a gas that rushes out of the nozzle.

Hose

Handle

Piercer

Carbon-dioxide canister

Water

Tube

Nozzle

Water extinguisher

Valve

Handle

Carbon dioxide vapor

Carbon dioxide liquid

Nozzle

Carbon dioxide extinguisher

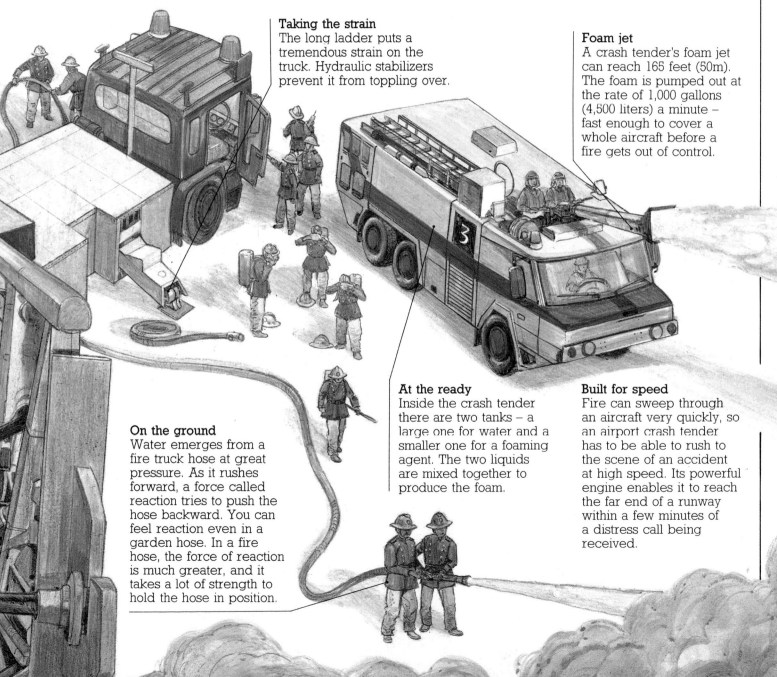

Taking the strain
The long ladder puts a tremendous strain on the truck. Hydraulic stabilizers prevent it from toppling over.

Foam jet
A crash tender's foam jet can reach 165 feet (50m). The foam is pumped out at the rate of 1,000 gallons (4,500 liters) a minute – fast enough to cover a whole aircraft before a fire gets out of control.

On the ground
Water emerges from a fire truck hose at great pressure. As it rushes forward, a force called reaction tries to push the hose backward. You can feel reaction even in a garden hose. In a fire hose, the force of reaction is much greater, and it takes a lot of strength to hold the hose in position.

At the ready
Inside the crash tender there are two tanks – a large one for water and a smaller one for a foaming agent. The two liquids are mixed together to produce the foam.

Built for speed
Fire can sweep through an aircraft very quickly, so an airport crash tender has to be able to rush to the scene of an accident at high speed. Its powerful engine enables it to reach the far end of a runway within a few minutes of a distress call being received.

45

DRILLING FOR OIL

Oil is essential for fueling countless kinds of machines, and also for providing the raw materials from which substances like plastics are made. Oil lies in great natural reservoirs underground. It is brought to the surface by drilling wells down to reach it. The oil is often under pressure, and it flows upward without any help once the well has been drilled. As the oil is removed, the speed of flow slows down. Water or gas is sometimes pumped back down the well to push more oil to the surface.

At one time, all the oil came from wells that were drilled on land. But as the thirst for oil has continued to grow, oil production has moved out to sea as well. Offshore oil rigs are some of the largest and most expensive structures ever built. They have to carry all the equipment and crew needed to find and produce oil. Each one is like a town built with steel and concrete. An offshore rig has its own power and water supply, accommodation blocks, helicopter pad, and first aid post. Most important of all, a rig has to be able to survive the severest storms. The huge legs beneath the water are designed to keep it stable in the most stormy conditions, and to stand up to corrosion caused by salty water.

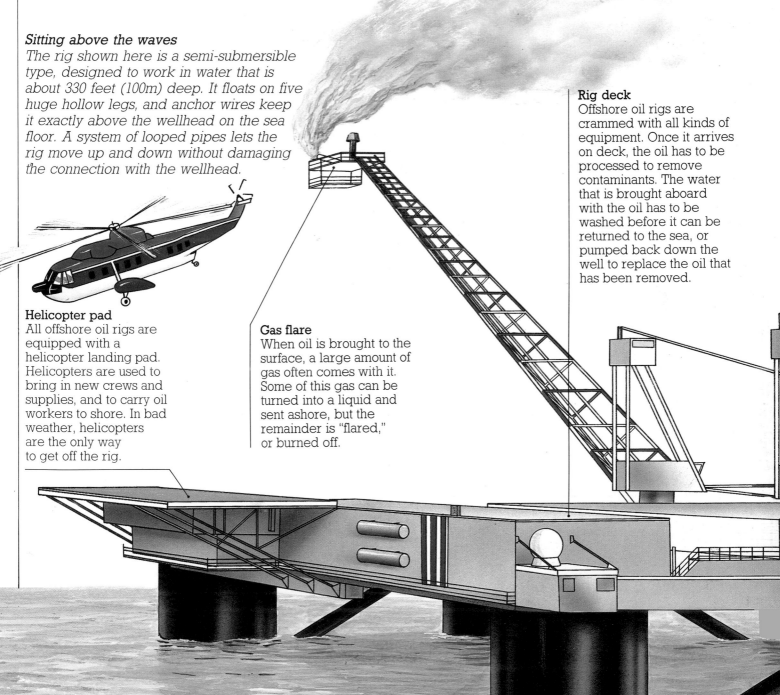

Sitting above the waves
The rig shown here is a semi-submersible type, designed to work in water that is about 330 feet (100m) deep. It floats on five huge hollow legs, and anchor wires keep it exactly above the wellhead on the sea floor. A system of looped pipes lets the rig move up and down without damaging the connection with the wellhead.

Helicopter pad
All offshore oil rigs are equipped with a helicopter landing pad. Helicopters are used to bring in new crews and supplies, and to carry oil workers to shore. In bad weather, helicopters are the only way to get off the rig.

Gas flare
When oil is brought to the surface, a large amount of gas often comes with it. Some of this gas can be turned into a liquid and sent ashore, but the remainder is "flared," or burned off.

Rig deck
Offshore oil rigs are crammed with all kinds of equipment. Once it arrives on deck, the oil has to be processed to remove contaminants. The water that is brought aboard with the oil has to be washed before it can be returned to the sea, or pumped back down the well to replace the oil that has been removed.

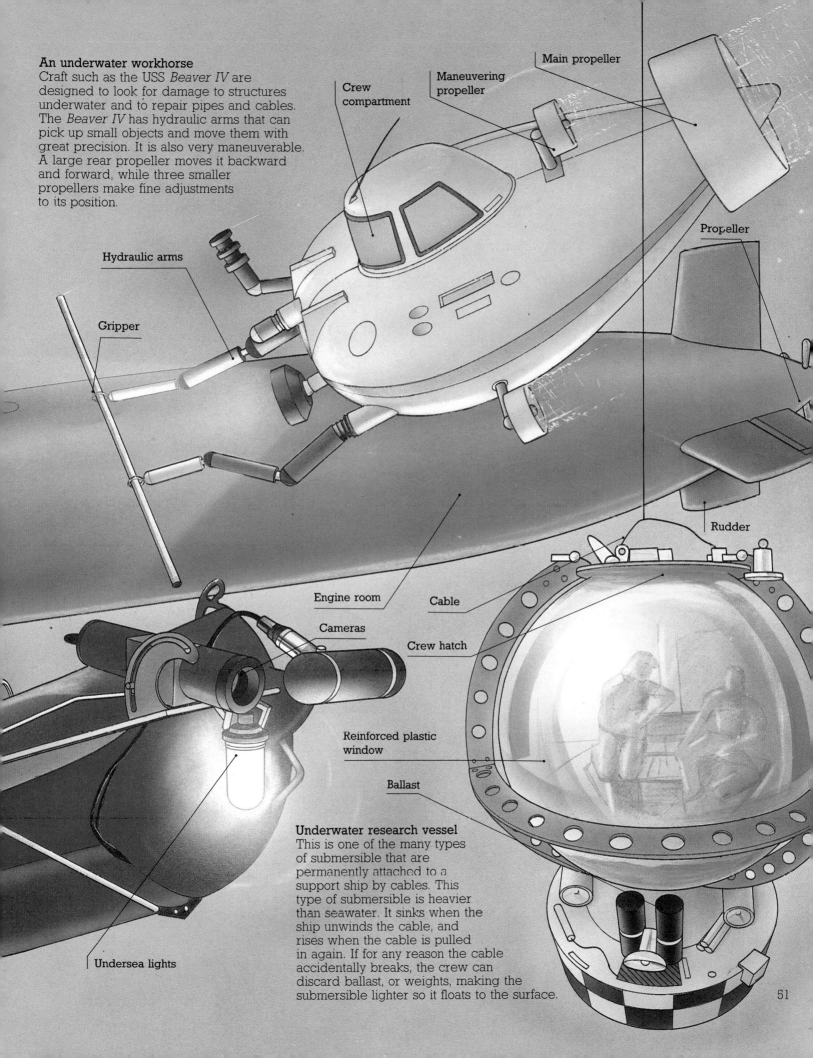

An underwater workhorse
Craft such as the USS *Beaver IV* are
designed to look for damage to structures
underwater and to repair pipes and cables.
The *Beaver IV* has hydraulic arms that can
pick up small objects and move them with
great precision. It is also very maneuverable.
A large rear propeller moves it backward
and forward, while three smaller
propellers make fine adjustments
to its position.

Crew
compartment

Maneuvering
propeller

Main propeller

Propeller

Hydraulic arms

Gripper

Rudder

Engine room

Cable

Cameras

Crew hatch

Reinforced plastic
window

Ballast

Undersea lights

Underwater research vessel
This is one of the many types
of submersible that are
permanently attached to a
support ship by cables. This
type of submersible is heavier
than seawater. It sinks when the
ship unwinds the cable, and
rises when the cable is pulled
in again. If for any reason the cable
accidentally breaks, the crew can
discard ballast, or weights, making the
submersible lighter so it floats to the surface.

51

METAL MOLES

Road and railway tunnels are cut by giant machines that push themselves forward underground, slicing away at the rock with huge rotating blades. A tunneling machine is like a long metal tube. At the front of the tube is the cutter head. Behind this, and inside the tube, are the hydraulic rams that make the machine move forward, conveyor belts that carry away the spoil, and a control cabin. A tunneling machine can move through soft rock at a speed of about 6½ feet (2m) an hour.

Tunneling machines are guided with lasers, to make sure that they follow the right course underground. In the longest tunnels, such as the Seikan Tunnel in Japan, the machines are used in pairs. They dig toward each other from opposite ends of the tunnel, following a precisely charted course. The laser guidance system makes sure that the two ends of the tunnel join exactly.

Tunneling machines

The machines that are used to cut the Channel Tunnel between England and France are about 100 feet (30m) long. Behind each one is a system of conveyor belts, pumps, ventilation pipes, and spoil wagons. This stretches back for 500 feet (150m).

Steel casing of tunneling machine

Spoil conveyor belt

Cutter head
At the front of the tunneling machine, a circular cutter head turns between two and four times every minute. Metal gouges on the head scrape away at the rock or clay.

Control cabin
Just behind the cutting head is a control cabin, equipped with a laser guidance system and closed-circuit television. The operator inside the cabin is protected by the steel casing of the tunneling machine.

Fundraising banquet in the Thames Tunnel, 1843

Hydraulic arm

Walkway

Lining the tunnel
As the cutter head slowly creeps forward, the hydraulic arms lift the concrete lining segments and place them in position against the tunnel wall. This seals the tunnel, stopping it from collapsing and preventing water from getting in.

Lining segments
The concrete lining segments are delivered on a conveyor belt to the hydraulic arms that will put them in position. When the tunneling machine is working at full speed, two complete rings of lining segments are put in position every hour.

Removing the spoil
In large tunneling machines, the broken rock is carried away from the cutter head first by a device like an Archimedean screw (page 8) and then by a conveyor belt. If the ground is waterlogged, the spoil is a thick liquid, which is pumped back out of the tunnel.

Air supply
Fresh air must be pumped in to reduce the amount of dust, and to allow the people operating the machines to breathe. It arrives through a large pipe at the top of the tunnel. Like all the pipes and conveyor belts, it has to be extended all the time to keep it close to the end of the tunnel.

53

Supplying the tunneling machine

Behind the tunneling machine, the newly cut tunnel is full of the equipment that delivers essential parts and removes spoil. The tunneling machine carries out most of its work automatically, and so very few people actually work underground. The tunnel's progress can be monitored on the surface by closed-circuit television.

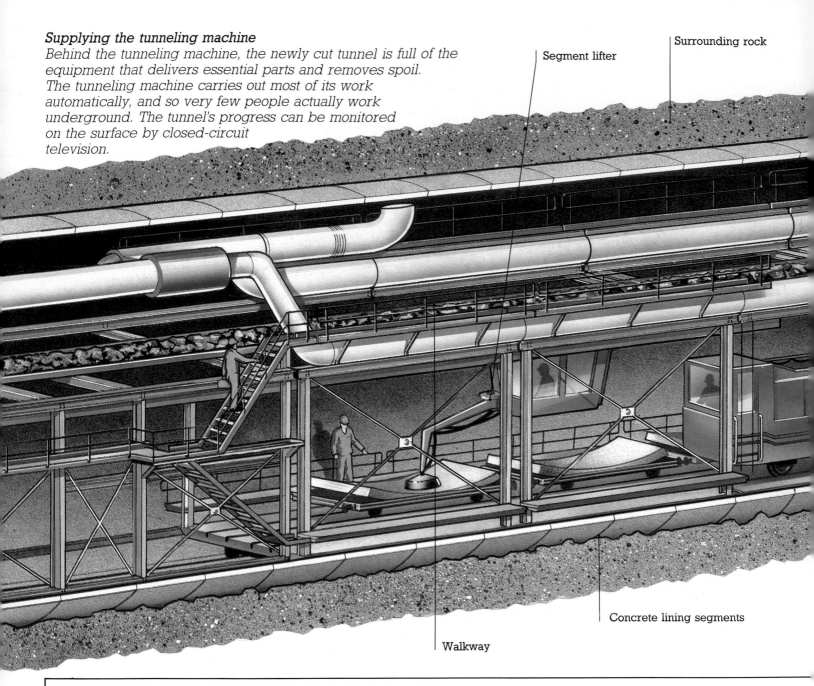

Segment lifter

Surrounding rock

Concrete lining segments

Walkway

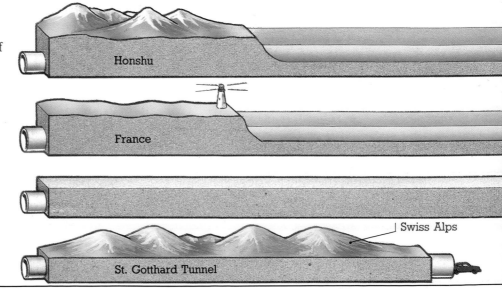

The world's longest tunnels

Railway tunnel
The Seikan Tunnel connects the islands of Honshu and Hokkaido in Japan.
33½ miles (54km)

Honshu

Channel Tunnel
Due for completion in 1993, this tunnel connects England and France.
31 miles (50km)

France

Subway tunnel
The Moscow Metro contains the world's longest stretch of subway tunnel.
19 miles (31km)

Road tunnel
The St. Gotthard Tunnel runs under the high mountains of the Swiss Alps.
10 miles (16.5km)

Swiss Alps

St. Gotthard Tunnel

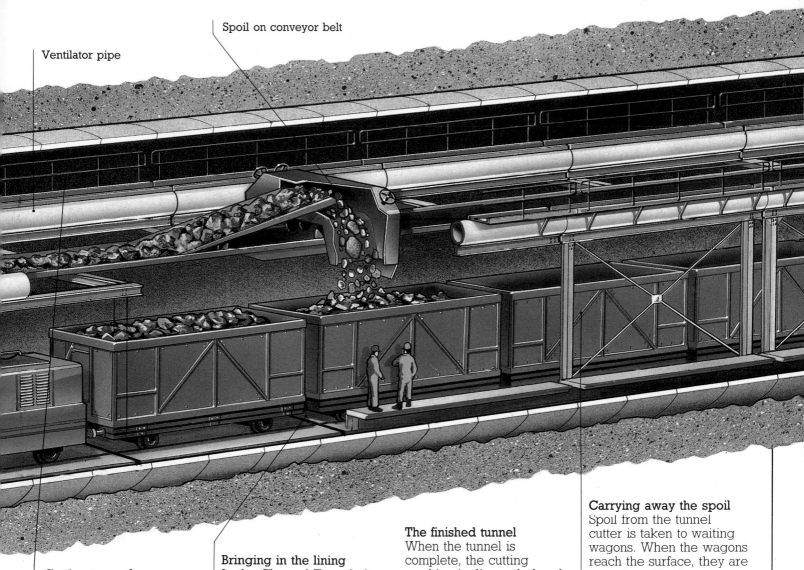

Ventilator pipe

Spoil on conveyor belt

Getting to work
The engineers who operate the tunneling machine reach the front of the machine by walkway. A rail car carries them back to the surface.

Bringing in the lining
In the Channel Tunnel, the concrete lining segments are 5 feet (1.5m) wide. Each tunnel cutting machine uses 550 tons of them every hour that it works.

The finished tunnel
When the tunnel is complete, the cutting machine is dismantled and other equipment is removed. A permanent rail track or road is laid on the floor of the tunnel, and lighting, emergency telephones, and ventilators are installed.

Carrying away the spoil
Spoil from the tunnel cutter is taken to waiting wagons. When the wagons reach the surface, they are turned upside down so that the spoil falls out. Each of the machines used to cut the Channel Tunnel produces up to 2,200 tons of spoil an hour, which has to be carried to the surface.

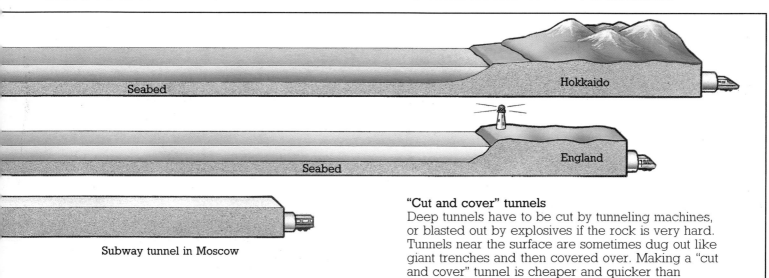

Seabed

Hokkaido

Seabed

England

Subway tunnel in Moscow

"Cut and cover" tunnels
Deep tunnels have to be cut by tunneling machines, or blasted out by explosives if the rock is very hard. Tunnels near the surface are sometimes dug out like giant trenches and then covered over. Making a "cut and cover" tunnel is cheaper and quicker than digging one deep down.

IN THE PICTURE

A modern SLR (single-lens reflex) camera is a marvel of precision engineering. Although it can be held easily, it contains thousands of separate components, all designed to make sure that the light entering the lens creates the best possible picture.

To take a photograph with an SLR camera, you first focus the lens by looking through the viewfinder. Some cameras now use electronics to do this for you. Next, you set the aperture. This adjusts the iris, which controls the amount of light that enters the camera. The bigger the aperture, the more light is let in. Most SLR cameras will then automatically select a shutter speed. This controls the exposure time, which is the length of the flash of light that enters the camera. This is important because a moving object will be blurred if the exposure is too long. Finally, you press the shutter release button.

The SLR Camera

With an SLR camera, the image you see through the viewfinder is the same image that falls on the film. Normally, the light that enters the camera through the lenses is reflected by the reflex mirror into the viewfinder. When you press the shutter, the reflex mirror swings upward to let the light reach the film.

Cameras in the past

The earliest cameras were little more than lightproof boxes. Instead of using a roll of film, they took pictures on plates. After a plate had been exposed, it had to be taken out of the camera and then developed straight away. Early plates were not very sensitive to light. Anybody wanting to have their photograph would have to sit absolutely still for up to a minute while the plate was exposed.

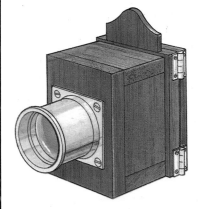

Fox Talbot camera

This camera was invented by William Fox Talbot in the 1830s. It was the first camera to produce photographs using negatives. This process allows many prints to be made from one exposure.

Brownie box camera

Early twentieth-century cameras such as the Brownie box made photography into a popular hobby. Like cameras today, the Brownie used a roll of film that was held between two spools.

Film advance lever

The film advance lever moves the film on by one frame after you have taken a photograph. Doing this also cocks the shutter, getting the camera ready to take the next picture. When all the film has been exposed, turning the rewind lever pulls the film back into its lightproof cassette. The film can then be taken out of the camera and processed.

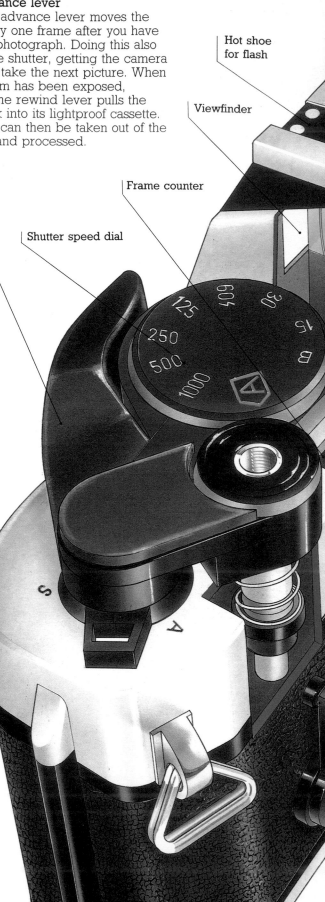

Hot shoe for flash

Viewfinder

Frame counter

Shutter speed dial

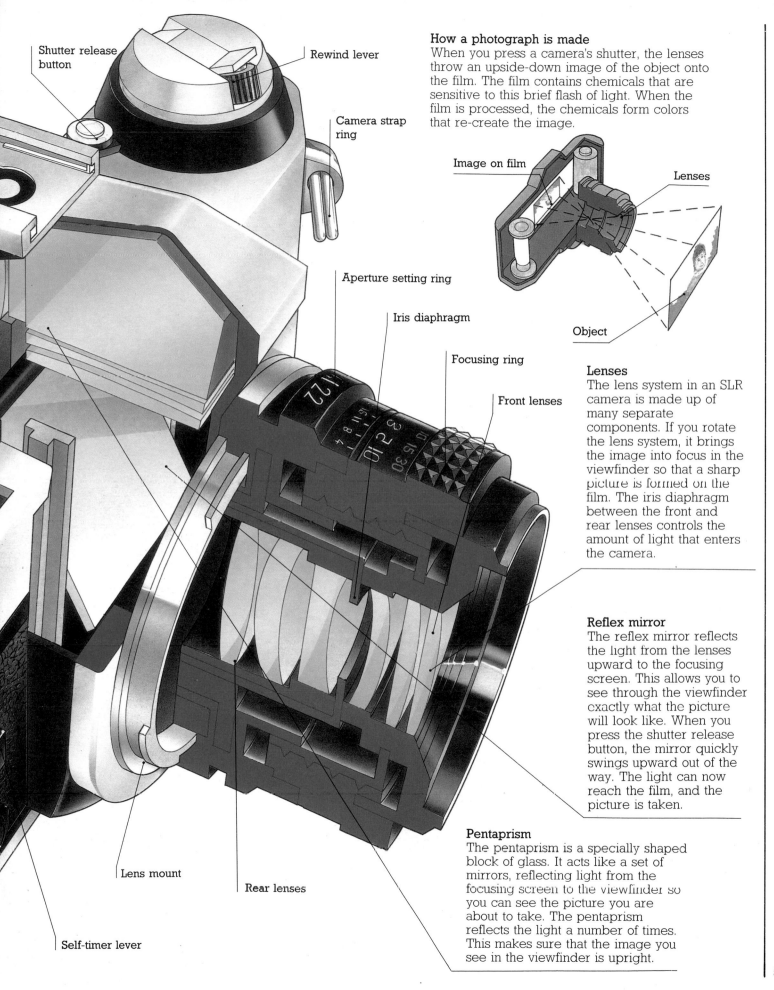

Shutter release button

Rewind lever

Camera strap ring

Aperture setting ring

Iris diaphragm

Focusing ring

Front lenses

Lens mount

Rear lenses

Self-timer lever

How a photograph is made

When you press a camera's shutter, the lenses throw an upside-down image of the object onto the film. The film contains chemicals that are sensitive to this brief flash of light. When the film is processed, the chemicals form colors that re-create the image.

Image on film

Lenses

Object

Lenses

The lens system in an SLR camera is made up of many separate components. If you rotate the lens system, it brings the image into focus in the viewfinder so that a sharp picture is formed on the film. The iris diaphragm between the front and rear lenses controls the amount of light that enters the camera.

Reflex mirror

The reflex mirror reflects the light from the lenses upward to the focusing screen. This allows you to see through the viewfinder exactly what the picture will look like. When you press the shutter release button, the mirror quickly swings upward out of the way. The light can now reach the film, and the picture is taken.

Pentaprism

The pentaprism is a specially shaped block of glass. It acts like a set of mirrors, reflecting light from the focusing screen to the viewfinder so you can see the picture you are about to take. The pentaprism reflects the light a number of times. This makes sure that the image you see in the viewfinder is upright.

ROBOTS AND ROBOTICS

Robots are the most versatile of all machines. They can be programmed to carry out a range of complex tasks, and they can run for long periods without anyone to supervize or control them directly. Robots are used to do work that is difficult, repetitive, or dangerous. With their electronic sensors, they can see or feel the objects they are working with. Signals from the sensors are passed to a robot's computer, which then makes any necessary adjustments to its position. Robots are the only machines that can respond to the world around them in this way. The robots shown here are working on a car assembly line. In some car factories, this process is carried out almost entirely by these automatic machines.

Non-stop workers

Millions of cars are produced every year around the world. A car assembly robot can work round the clock, carrying out intricate work like spot welding with great accuracy, its movements controlled by a computer program.

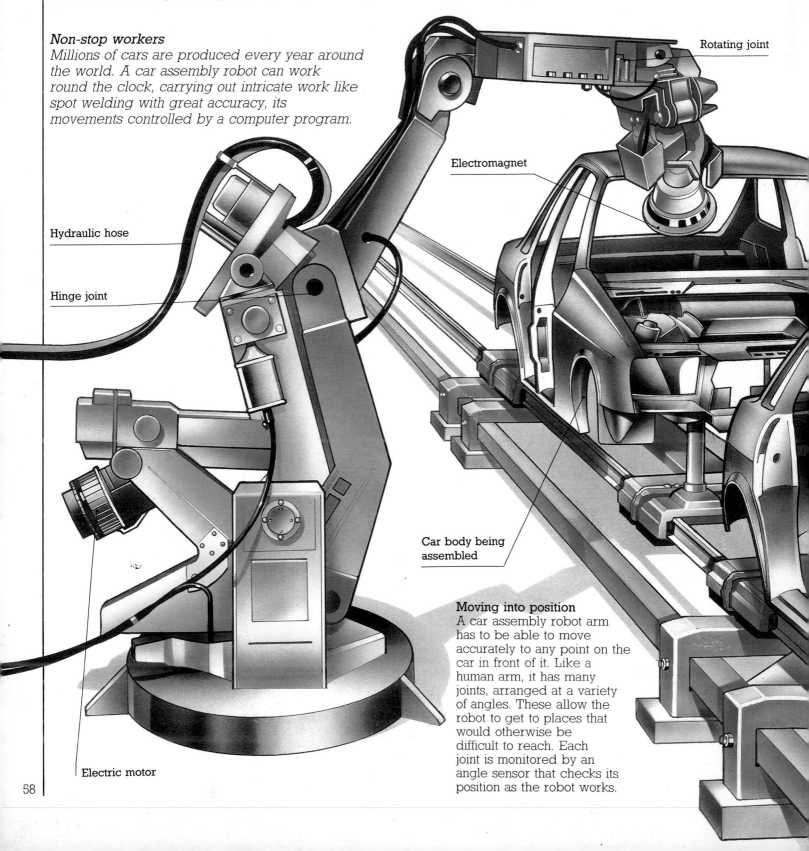

Rotating joint

Electromagnet

Hydraulic hose

Hinge joint

Car body being assembled

Electric motor

Moving into position

A car assembly robot arm has to be able to move accurately to any point on the car in front of it. Like a human arm, it has many joints, arranged at a variety of angles. These allow the robot to get to places that would otherwise be difficult to reach. Each joint is monitored by an angle sensor that checks its position as the robot works.

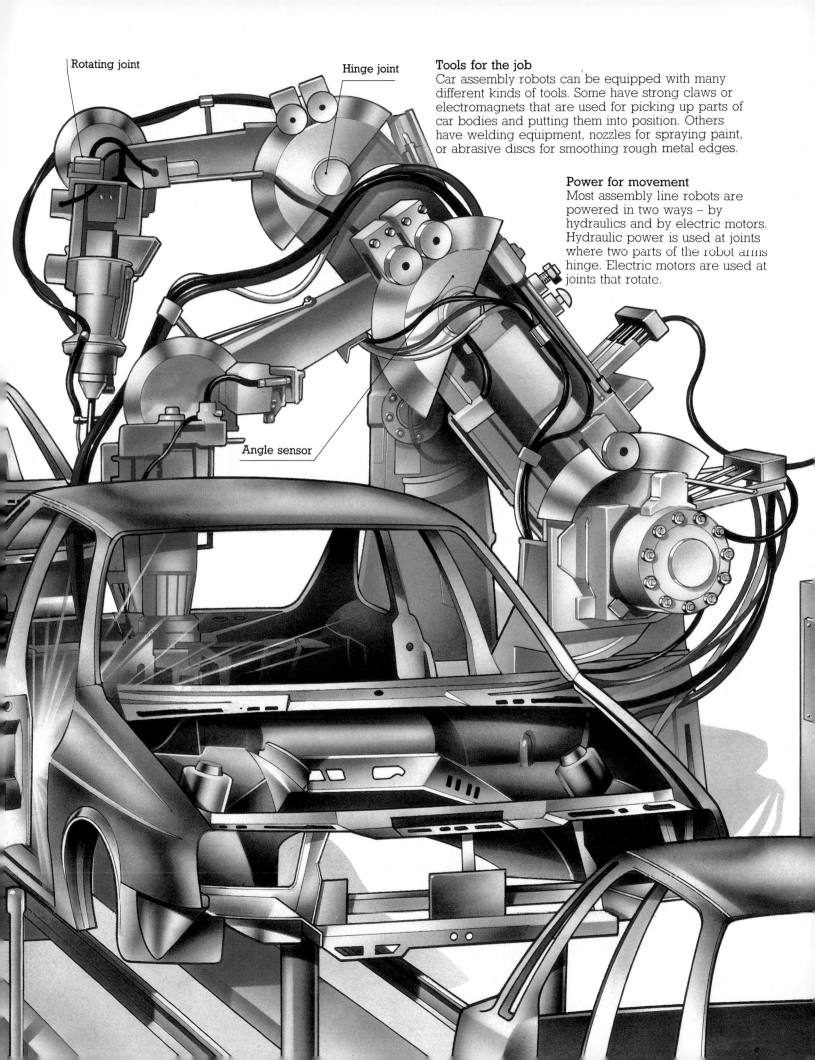

Rotating joint

Hinge joint

Angle sensor

Tools for the job
Car assembly robots can be equipped with many different kinds of tools. Some have strong claws or electromagnets that are used for picking up parts of car bodies and putting them into position. Others have welding equipment, nozzles for spraying paint, or abrasive discs for smoothing rough metal edges.

Power for movement
Most assembly line robots are powered in two ways – by hydraulics and by electric motors. Hydraulic power is used at joints where two parts of the robot arms hinge. Electric motors are used at joints that rotate.

The world of robots

If you want to see a robot in action, you probably do not need to look any further than your own home. Many household devices, including washing machines and microwave ovens, now work robotically. Once you have selected a program and switched them on, the devices control themselves through their microelectronic circuitry. These programmable household machines are the simplest kind of robots. In the future, more advanced robots will carry out all sorts of tasks in homes, factories – as well as in the far reaches of space!

Man and machine

Together, your arm and hand have over 25 joints. This allows you to make many different movements. By comparison, robot arms are quite simple. They usually have no more than about six joints. Despite this difference, human arms and robot arms work in much the same way. Each joint has its own power supply.

Paired muscles flex and extend joint

Joints in hand and wrist

Bone

Elbow joint

Hydraulic hose

Joint

Joint

Hydraulic hose

Joint

Robot arms are usually stronger but less flexible than human arms

Control center

The control center is the robot's "brain." It contains the computer program that guides the robot as it works. The program for a paint-spraying robot tells the robot where to paint and how long to spray each part for. It also makes the robot arm move as quickly as possible from one point to the next.

Hydraulic hose

Paint hose

Paint-spraying nozzle

Paint hose

Learning the work

Robots that work on car assembly lines are sometimes "taught" how to do their work. First, a robot is guided through a series of movements by its "teacher." The robot's control center then remembers the movements, and the robot carries them out as many times as required.

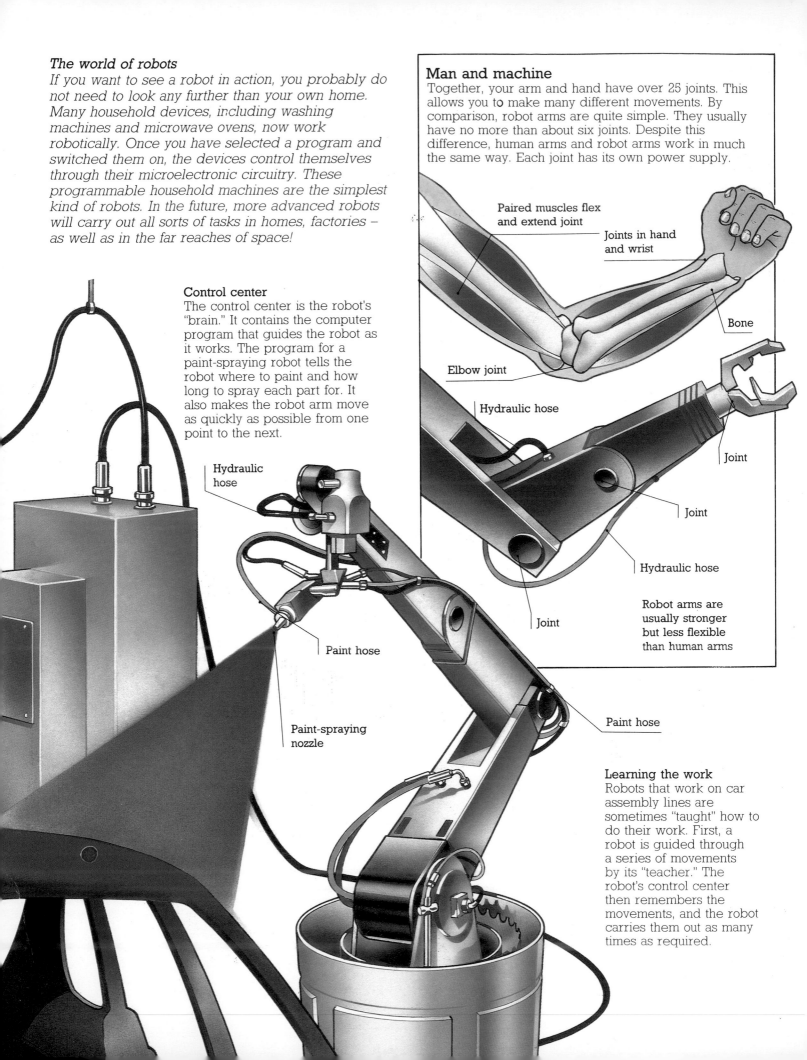

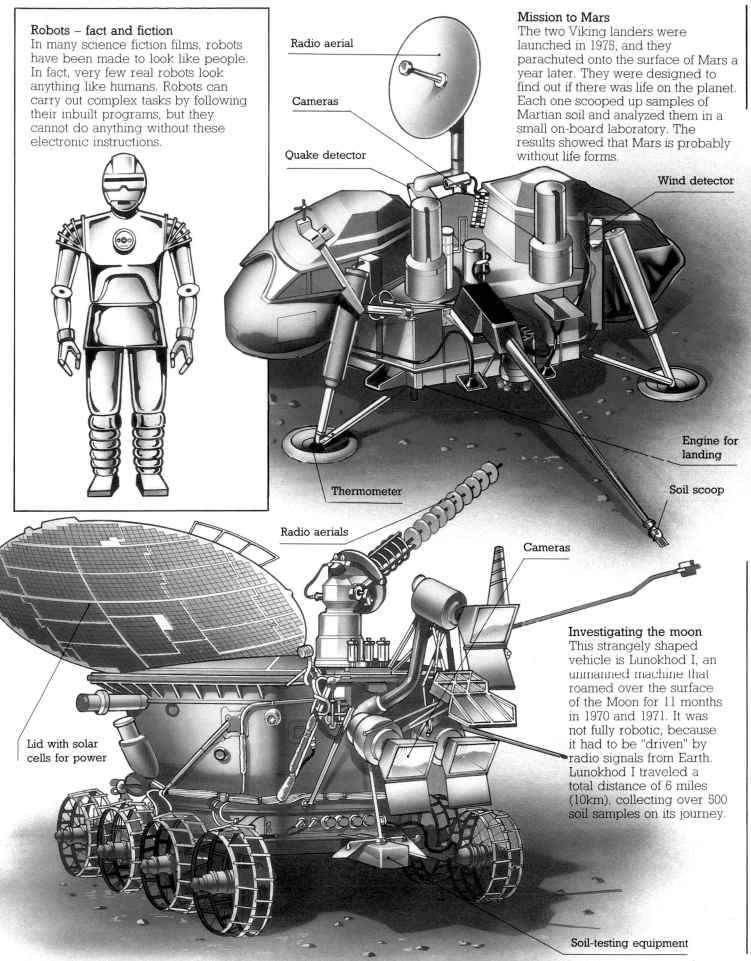

Robots – fact and fiction

In many science fiction films, robots have been made to look like people. In fact, very few real robots look anything like humans. Robots can carry out complex tasks by following their inbuilt programs, but they cannot do anything without these electronic instructions.

Radio aerial

Cameras

Quake detector

Mission to Mars

The two Viking landers were launched in 1975, and they parachuted onto the surface of Mars a year later. They were designed to find out if there was life on the planet. Each one scooped up samples of Martian soil and analyzed them in a small on-board laboratory. The results showed that Mars is probably without life forms.

Wind detector

Engine for landing

Soil scoop

Thermometer

Radio aerials

Cameras

Investigating the moon

This strangely shaped vehicle is Lunokhod I, an unmanned machine that roamed over the surface of the Moon for 11 months in 1970 and 1971. It was not fully robotic, because it had to be "driven" by radio signals from Earth. Lunokhod I traveled a total distance of 6 miles (10km), collecting over 500 soil samples on its journey.

Lid with solar cells for power

Soil-testing equipment

PERPETUAL MOTION

Imagine a machine that runs forever. It never needs refueling and never runs down, and as long as it is carefully built, it will go on working day after day, year after year, century after century. Can such a machine be built? Unfortunately, the answer to this question is "no." The scientific laws that govern all machines make it quite clear that you cannot get something for nothing. A machine needs energy to overcome friction and to do work. This energy cannot be created. Instead, it has to be provided, usually in the form of muscle power or fuel.

In the past, the laws of mechanics were not fully

The perpetual spinning wheel

This perpetual motion device featured a wheel divided into compartments, with a metal ball in each one. The balls rolled outward on one side of a wheel, and this was meant to produce the force that turned the wheel. Although a popular idea with inventors, it never worked.

The self-propelling cart

In this machine, a heavy ball was meant to keep rolling down a slope in a metal container. The container could swivel so that the ball never reached the bottom of the slope. This movement was meant to be transferred through gears to an axle, driving the cart along. In reality, the cart would have come to a halt within seconds.

A wondrous invention?

Some inventors went to great lengths in their quest to achieve perpetual motion. This complicated and impressive piece of machinery was designed in the seventeenth century. In theory, it was powered by the weight of wooden balls. The weight of the balls was meant to turn a device like a waterwheel. When each ball reached the foot of the wheel, it was supposed to roll to the bottom of an auger, which would lift it up to the top of the wheel again. The moving wheel would power the auger through a system of gears.

That, at least, was how the inventor thought it would work. However, he obviously forgot all about friction. The machine's many gears and bearings would have produced so much friction that it would have taken a lot of pushing to make it work. The moment the pushing stopped, the machine would have come to a standstill.

Auger

understood, and many inventors were convinced that perpetual (constant) motion was possible. Thousands of designs appeared for perpetual motion machines. Some inventors were so sure that their machines were going to work that they included special brakes to stop them from running out of control!

Doomed to failure

Perpetual motion machines were not always designed by genuine inventors. In times gone by, some people made money by showing fake "perpetual motion machines." These had a source of power hidden in the machine.

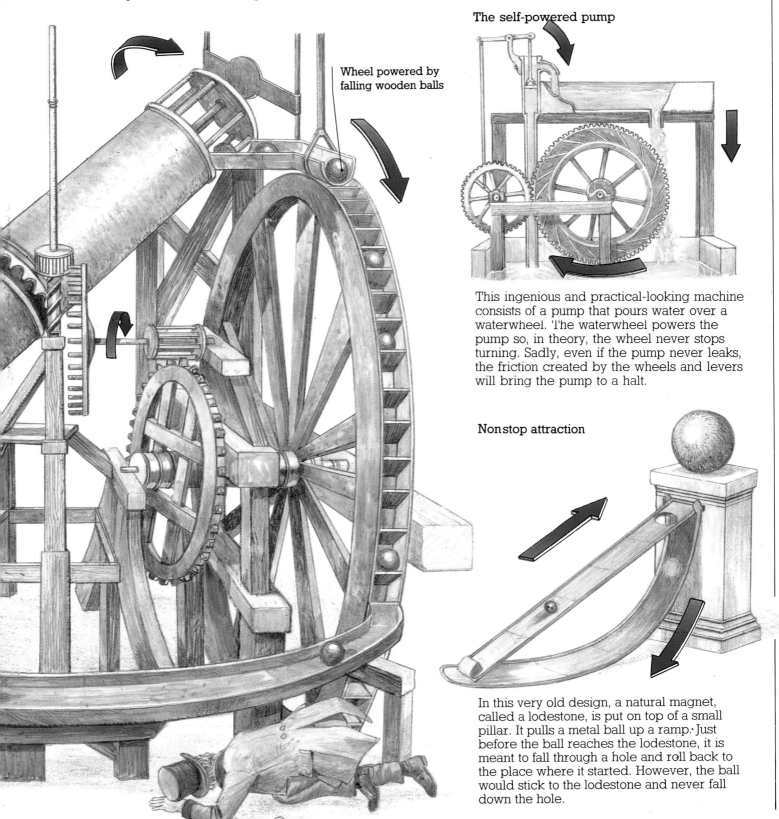

Wheel powered by falling wooden balls

The self-powered pump

This ingenious and practical-looking machine consists of a pump that pours water over a waterwheel. The waterwheel powers the pump so, in theory, the wheel never stops turning. Sadly, even if the pump never leaks, the friction created by the wheels and levers will bring the pump to a halt.

Nonstop attraction

In this very old design, a natural magnet, called a lodestone, is put on top of a small pillar. It pulls a metal ball up a ramp. Just before the ball reaches the lodestone, it is meant to fall through a hole and roll back to the place where it started. However, the ball would stick to the lodestone and never fall down the hole.